TRIUMPHING IN TRUTH

TRANSFORMING TRIALS INTO TESTIMONIES

ACE ASPIRAS

CONTENTS

INTRODUCTION

My world felt like a relentless storm. The echoes of past traumas seemed to constantly hover, casting long shadows, until a newfound purpose emerged—reinvigorating weary souls. On February 24, 2020, I found myself among a sea of mourners at the Staples Center, all gathered to pay homage to basketball legend Kobe Bryant and his daughter, Gigi. Little did I know that this day, saturated with shared global grief, would kickstart a profound personal transformation. That same evening, transitioning from the familiar grounds of the NICU, I entered the uncertain terrains of the ICU. In Room 3113, a woman with stubborn lungs, almost resistant to life, became my responsibility. Each patient narrated stories of vulnerability and strength, but the woman in room 3113 left an imprint on my heart.

It was naive to think that the emotional weight of such a profession could remain separate from my private existence. Then, as I was sitting at a Warriors-Lakers game, a single call altered the course of my life. The news relayed the first community-acquired COVID-19 case in the U.S. This wasn't just a headline; it felt like a cosmic push, or perhaps divine intervention, steering me towards a redefined mission. Faced with the heart-wrenching scenes of individuals on the brink, many facing the abyss alone, a prayer surged from within: "Lord, grant me the strength to guide these souls through their darkest hours."

This invisible enemy transformed my every day into a turbulent battlefield. Navigating through the maze of uncertainties, suppressing innate fears, and absorbing waves of emotions, I barely realized its toll on my spirit.

Feelings of agony, bitterness, and anger soon began to overpower me as they cast their debilitating shadows. Empowerment seemed impossible while loneliness slowly chipped away at me. Despite God's gentle promptings to find comfort in Him, shame and anxiety often won.

Yet, even in the most tragic hours, the parable of the Good Shepherd, tirelessly seeking the lone lost sheep, resonated deeply within me. Through my roles—as a son, a husband, and a father—I witnessed God's boundless affection. At times when my spiritual reserves weakened, He ensured that aid was never far. From nature's wisdom, His message was clear: "A tree rooted beside a stream fears not the fiercest sun." My heart, anchored in forgiveness and mercy, should never remain trapped in the past.

Through subtle and grand gestures, God transformed my adversities into affirming stories of His steadfast love. I am Ace—a warrior refined by His celestial grace. A beacon of patience and sobriety, I stand with pride, forever humbled by His benevolence, fortified by the Holy Spirit, and perpetually grateful for the sacrifices of Jesus. Each breath I take is a testament to the spirit's enduring guidance. This epic journey has illuminated the importance of endless growth and reflection. Cultivating a growth-oriented mindset, deriving insights from past journeys, fostering dreams, and elevating those around us form the core of our shared human experience. We often struggle with understanding our purpose, navigating challenges, and seeking meaning.

My intent is not just to share a story but to kindle a flame in your heart, to prompt you to go deep within, confront your shadows, and emerge with a renewed sense of purpose and enlightenment. My intent for this book was to draw upon universal truths and divine wisdom, reflect life's challenges, and have it act as a handbook for personal growth. Highlighting that while our journeys are unique, the themes of truth, transformation, and testimony resonate with us all.

Trilogy of Triumph

Truth, transformation, and testimony are what I call the Trilogy of Triumph. This methodology has not only withstood the test of time but has proven its relevance repeatedly across different generations.

Truth is about recognizing who we are, the pure version of ourselves that remains constant even as life changes. It's about understanding our deepest desires, fears, ambitions, and emotions, undistorted by societal pressures or external influences. The first step towards any meaningful transformation is recognizing and accepting our truth, no matter how uncomfortable or confronting it might be.

Transformation follows truth. Once we understand who we are and where we stand, we can take steps towards positive change. This is not about becoming someone new but instead allowing the best version of ourselves to come forth. It's a process, often challenging but always rewarding. Each step in this transformation will bring us closer to realizing our potential.

Finally, there's testimony. Sharing our stories, challenges, triumphs, and even defeats is crucial. Why? Because our stories have power. They inspire, they resonate, and they forge connections. Testifying our journey validates our experiences and guides others on similar paths.

Spirituality, Self-growth, and Personal Freedom

Humans have been curious creatures for eons, constantly probing the physical, mental, and spiritual realms. Curiosity has led to countless quests for knowledge, power, peace, or enlightenment. One aspect of all these pursuits is the connection between spirituality, self-growth, and personal freedom.

Spirituality, often mistaken as religious practices, is broader. It's about understanding our place in the grand scheme of things and recognizing a force greater than ourselves. This spiritual awareness often leads to self-growth. As we start understanding the broader universe, we also realize our potential.

Hand-in-hand with self-growth comes personal freedom. Not in the physical sense alone, but the freedom to think, feel, express, and be. It's about breaking the chains—be it of societal norms, self-imposed limitations, or external pressures—and experiencing the exhilaration of true liberty.

From Ma'at to Taoism, from tribal rituals to yoga, from the serene assurances of Christianity to various other faiths and practices, a singular, universal truth emerges: the human spirit innately seeks peace. This universal quest emphasizes our shared humanity, a binding thread that connects us across generations. While our expressions of this quest might differ, the heart of it remains unchanged: a yearning for inner stillness, a sanctuary within, where the soul finds peace.

In the forthcoming chapters, we'll dive deeper into these facets, exploring them through various lenses and understanding how they collectively form the backbone of our journey towards inner peace and self-awareness. As you turn these pages, I hope you find comfort in shared experiences, strength in collective wisdom, and a renewed energy to embrace your own path with courage and conviction. Let this motivate you from introspection to action, challenges to triumphs, and fleeting moments to eternal legacies. Welcome to a voyage of discovery, reflection, and profound transformation!

Truth

1

—·—

UNEARTHING YOUR CORE TRUTH

Authenticity stands as a beacon in the maze of life, leading us toward genuine contentment and self-realization. However, in an ever-evolving society with ever-evolving expectations and social molds, maintaining our inherent authenticity may prove challenging in today's fast-paced environment. Trends, ads, peer pressure, and peer expectations all aspire to take over our identities—quickly leading us away from who we are as individuals.

This chapter centers around the sacred pursuit of genuine authenticity—not something external but towards our roots and inner being. Too often, it's assumed we need to change to fit in this chaotic world. Yet, the more profound truth suggests otherwise: instead of becoming someone or something else to find our place among its chaos, rather than becoming someone or something it should be about unbecoming everything that doesn't feel authentic to you and shedding layers that have accumulated over time, remembering, rediscovery and returning should be key parts.

Reflect for a moment on the metaphor of a sculpture. Each block of stone has a masterpiece hidden within, waiting to be revealed. The sculptor's job isn't to add anything but to chip away the excess, revealing the work of art that's always been there. Similarly, in many ways, our life's task is to peel back the layers of imposed identity and unearth our genuine self, the masterpiece within.

The further we drift from our authentic nature, the more turbulent our internal world becomes. We may achieve societal accolades, amass material success, or even gain the admiration of peers. Still, without genuine authenticity, a void persists. It's like wearing a mask so long that we forget the face underneath. The mask might be beautiful, impressive, or even intimidating, but it's not truly us.

Returning to your true nature may seem complicated, but its challenges can be managed effortlessly. Many have embarked on this journey before us, sharing their wisdom, experiences, and insights that can light our way back home. With introspection, mindfulness practice, spirituality, and practicality guiding our way, we can navigate our way back home—our authentic core self.

This chapter is a compass for those brave souls willing to undertake this journey. It's a guide that intertwines timeless wisdom with actionable steps, ensuring our voyage toward our core truth is enlightening and grounded in reality. So, let's begin, with open hearts and minds, on this sacred journey of return.

Societal Expectations and Their Influences

From the moment we take our first breath, the world around us begins to mold our perceptions, dictating, often subtly, what's acceptable, what's admirable, and what's frowned upon. Every society, every culture, and family has its unique set of unwritten rules, norms, and values. These forces, some clear to recognize and others more subtle, greatly influence our behaviors, decisions, and beliefs.

Let's take a brief journey across the world. Eastern cultures prioritize family and societal cohesion; "the nail that sticks out gets hammered down" describes this philosophy that permeates many Asian countries. Individual desires and ambitions often take second place in familial duties and expectations. Meanwhile, Western cultures, emphasizing individualism, often encourage self-expression and independence—though this comes with its own pressures, such as independence from established norms or "standing out."

Within our cultural backgrounds, our families further shape our perspectives. Academic excellence may be encouraged and expected in certain households; others are expected to follow family traditions or take over family businesses. Although often well-intended, familial expectations can act like golden cages, full of love but restrictive nonetheless.

But why do we, as thinking-feeling beings, so often fall in line, molding our desires and dreams based on these external pressures?

Part of the answer lies in our basic need for acceptance and belonging. From our early days as hunter-gatherers, being part of the tribe was crucial for survival. Those who didn't conform faced exclusion, which back then often equated to a death sentence. This deep-seated fear of exclusion remains embedded in our psyche, urging us to conform, even when conformity feels like a straightjacket.

Another reason behind our tendency to conform is societal pressures pervasive in everyday life, from media consumption and casual conversations with family and friends all the way up to formal school settings. Constant exposure reinforces societal norms, making them seem as natural and permanent as the passing seasons.

However, conformity has its costs. With each unfulfilled dream and each silenced voice, a piece of our authentic self fades into oblivion. The mask we wear becomes heavier, and the disconnect between our inner world and external persona widens. This division can lead to feelings of unfulfillment, restlessness, and sometimes even resentment.

Let me be clear: not all societal norms are harmful. Many exist for the greater good, fostering harmony, mutual respect, and collective well-being. However, the challenge lies in discerning which expectations align with our true nature and which ones merely bind us in chains of inauthenticity. Recognizing, understanding, and navigating these influences is crucial to our journey back to genuine authenticity.

The Masks We Wear

We often have to switch roles, wearing different masks for different stages of life. Some of these masks are adorned by choice, while others seem forced upon us by circumstances or societal pressures. These masks serve various purposes, whether it's the confident executive mask we wear at work, the nurturing parent at home, or the always-happy influencer persona on social media.

For instance, professionalism might dictate that we keep our personal problems at the door, presenting a calm exterior even when our inner world is in turmoil. This mask serves a purpose: it ensures smooth functioning in a corporate environment. It can even be a protective mechanism, shielding our vulnerabilities from potential scrutiny or judgment.

In family settings, particularly as parents or caregivers, we might wear the mask of the "pillar of strength," always available, understanding, and patient. This mask is worn out of love and responsibility, out of the desire to provide stability and security to our loved ones.

And then there's the world of social media, a space that has increasingly blurred the lines between reality and perception. Here, we present an image of perpetual happiness, success, and contentment, filtering out the moments of doubt or sadness—often to fit in or be liked—or perhaps create a narrative that appears more appealing than our true selves.

But what lies underneath these masks, and why do we feel compelled to wear them in the first place?

On a practical level, these personas help us navigate the complexities of different social situations. They provide some degree of order, a set of guidelines on how to behave and what to expect in return. Moreover, they can also act as protective barriers, guarding our true selves against potential hurt, criticism, or rejection.

However, the continuous act of mask-wearing comes at an emotional and spiritual cost. It demands energy, constant vigilance, and, at times, a suppression of our genuine feelings and desires. Over time, this can lead to exhaustion, alienation, and disconnection, not just from the world around us but, more importantly, from our own selves. The weight of these masks can cloud our understanding of who we truly are, casting shadows over our authentic selves.

Spiritually, this dissonance between our external persona and inner essence can be uncomfortable and create barriers in our quest for deeper meaning, purpose, and connection. With each layer we add on top of ourselves comes greater difficulty connecting deeply—to ourselves, others, and the larger universe.

Although some masks can be essential and beneficial, we must regularly assess their authenticity and necessity. By understanding why we wear each one and their ramifications on us individually, conscious decisions can be made regarding shedding those that no longer serve us and welcome in the real version of ourselves with acceptance and love.

Why Rediscovering Authenticity Matters

Rediscovering authenticity in today's fast-paced world is more than an idealistic sentiment; it is vital for our well-being and holistic health. Being authentic means more than simply being true to oneself—it involves aligning our actions, thoughts, and words with our core beliefs and values—This alignment is crucial for our sense of self and emotional well-being.

Let's first examine the undeniable link between authenticity and mental health. Cognitive dissonance occurs when we are inauthentic, wear masks, or act out of sync with our true nature. Our mind constantly juggles who we are and who we project ourselves to be. This constant tug of war can manifest as stress, anxiety, or even depressive symptoms over time. On the contrary, authenticity eliminates this inner conflict, allowing for peace and clarity.

Moreover, authenticity plays a pivotal role in our relationships. Genuine interactions, free from judgment, allow for deeper connections. When we are our true selves, we attract people who resonate with our core, leading to more fulfilling and lasting bonds. On the other hand, relationships built on facades are often shallow and can crumble under the slightest pressure.

Authenticity also enhances our self-esteem and confidence. Every time we act authentically, it's an affirmation of our worth and our values. Over time, this builds a strong foundation of self-worth, making us resilient to external criticisms or judgments. We no longer seek validation from the world outside because we find it within ourselves.

From a holistic health perspective, living in alignment with our core truth benefits our minds and bodies. Emotional turmoil and mental stress, often from inauthenticity, can manifest as physical ailments. In contrast, when we are at peace with ourselves, our body functions more optimally, our sleep improves, our immune system strengthens, and we generally experience better health outcomes.

Finally, authenticity paves the way for genuine happiness and contentment. It's not about the fleeting joys of external achievements but the deep, abiding happiness that comes from living true to oneself. It's the joy of waking up each day, knowing that we are in harmony with ourselves, free from the exhausting charade of pretense.

The journey back to authenticity can be challenging in a world that often dictates who we should be, what we desire, and how we should act. But it's a journey worth undertaking. In embracing our authentic selves, we find the freedom to be, love, and truly live. Practical tools and self-reflection can guide us in this quest, helping us shed layers of conditioning and expectation bringing us closer to our essence and the profound peace and happiness it offers.

Reconnecting with One's Truth

As much as the world around us shifts and transforms, one immovable constant remains: Our inherent truth. This fundamental aspect defines who we truly are beyond societal expectations or roles we may assume; just like snowflakes are unique, so is each person with their unique pattern and essence.

The concept of 'innate truth' isn't new-age jargon; it's rooted in the understanding that we are born with unique tendencies, inclinations, and passions. Think of it as the compass needle of your soul, always pointing towards what feels most authentic and right for you. While the world may sometimes lead us astray with its magnetic distractions, our innate truth remains steadfast, awaiting our recognition and embrace.

On this journey back to truth, introspection becomes our most trusted ally. A profound way to start is by revisiting our childhood memories. Often, in childhood innocence, we were closest to our genuine selves before the layers of societal conditioning set in. Remember the activities that brought joy, the passions that ignited your heart, and the dreams that seemed as vast as the sky. Those weren't just fleeting moments but glimpses of your innate truth.

Yet, as life progresses, we sometimes drift away from this core, constructing walls around our true selves for protection or acceptance. Though seemingly secure, these walls are the barriers that prevent us from living our authentic lives. Addressing fears, insecurities, and "should haves" that shape our actions is paramount if you want a meaningful life experience—be sure to ask yourself, "Am I doing it because it feels right or because it is what others expect of me?".

The power of past experiences to limit us from living our authentic selves should also be noted here; internalized narratives from childhood experiences might prevent one from fully exploring one's true passions and accepting all parts of one's truth as an authentic identity. Being conscious, acknowledging, addressing, and healing these old wounds will allow one to embrace our truth completely.

However, reconnecting with one's innate truth isn't a one-off event but a continuous journey of self-discovery. It involves tuning in, listening to that inner voice, and having the courage to follow its guidance. It's about shedding the layers of expectations, past hurts, and societal norms to stand confidently in one's authentic light.

Remember that the path isn't always linear. There will be moments of doubt, setbacks, and external pressures. But with each step taken in alignment with our truth, we move closer to a life of genuine happiness, purpose, and unparalleled freedom.

The Power of Silence and Solitude

Silence and solitude have become rare commodities in our bustling, noisy world, where every second is often inundated with countless notifications, sounds, and demands. Yet, in these moments of quiet introspection and undisturbed calm, we truly begin to meet ourselves, listen deeply, and connect to our core.

Silence is more than the absence of noise; it's the presence of profound inner peace. It's a sanctuary where the outer world's demands fade, and we are left with our thoughts, feelings, and reflections. In this space, we can start to discern the subtle stirrings of our soul, those soft whispers that often get drowned out in daily life's noise.

Imagine, for a moment, the vast expanse of a calm lake, untouched and unruffled. Our mind can resemble this serene picture when we engage in intentional silence. It becomes a mirror, reflecting our most authentic self, not hidden by the ripples of external influences or inner turmoil. And it's in this clarity that profound insights and realizations can emerge.

Solitude, on the other hand, is the intentional act of spending time alone. Unlike loneliness, a feeling of emotional isolation, solitude is a chosen state of being. It is a sanctuary where one can temporarily step away from roles, responsibilities, and societal masks, creating a space to just "be." Here, free from judgment or expectation, we can reconnect with our authentic self, our innate truth.

Embracing solitude doesn't necessarily mean retreating to a mountaintop or forest (though those are wonderful options). It can be as simple as dedicating a time each day to sit alone with your thoughts, perhaps in a quiet corner of your home or a peaceful spot in a nearby park. It's about creating intentional pockets of time where you're present with yourself, undistracted.

Both silence and solitude serve as portals to deeper self-awareness. They strip away the noise and allow us to tune into our internal frequency. Over time, as we cultivate these practices, they become less of an escape from the world and more of a bridge to our true selves. We begin to discern our genuine desires, values, and inclinations, untainted by external pressures.

In this age of constant stimuli and connectivity, finding time and space for silence and solitude is both a luxury and a necessity for our mental and spiritual well-being. They are powerful tools, enabling us to journey inward, discover our truths, and return to the world with renewed clarity, purpose, and authenticity.

Exercises for Introspective Reflection

In our quest for authenticity, practical tools can guide our exploration inward, helping us unearth buried feelings, aspirations, and truths. Introspective reflection, aided by specific exercises, can open doors within ourselves we didn't even know existed. Here are some actionable techniques to help guide this inner journey:

Journaling Prompts for Self-Discovery:

Journaling is a therapeutic exercise that aids in self-awareness and emotional processing. Putting pen to paper gives our internal dialogues a tangible form, allowing for deeper analysis and understanding. Consider starting with these prompts:

- List five moments in your life when you felt most alive. What were you doing, and who were you with?

- Describe a belief you once held firmly but have since let go. What led to this change?

- Write a letter to your younger self. What wisdom and advice would you share?

- Imagine spending a day doing what you love. What does this day look like from start to finish?

Mindfulness and Meditation Practices:

Meditation, in its many forms, is a pathway to inner stillness and heightened self-awareness. Mindfulness, a form of meditation, centers on being fully present in the moment.

- Begin with simple breathing exercises. Close your eyes and focus solely on your breath. Inhale deeply through the nose, hold for a moment, and then exhale slowly through the mouth.

- Progress to guided meditation sessions, available on numerous apps or online platforms, tailored for self-discovery and grounding.

- Practice daily mindfulness by immersing yourself entirely in routine tasks, whether savoring a meal, listening to music, or feeling the water droplets during a shower. Embrace each sensation and emotion.

Physical Exercises for Grounding and Self-Connection:

Our bodies often hold clues about our inner states. Physical activities enhance our health and foster a deeper connection with our inner self.

- **Nature Walks**: Nature has an innate healing and grounding quality. Walking in natural settings—a forest, beach, or park—can provide clarity and a sense of connection. Try walking barefoot on grass or sand, absorbing the earth's energy.

- **Yoga**: More than just a physical discipline, yoga intertwines the body, mind, and spirit. Asanas (poses) and pranayama (breath control) guide us inward, fostering self-awareness and tranquility.

- **Dance**: Play your favorite music and let your body move freely. Dance is a form of expressive therapy, allowing emotions and energy to flow unbridled.

While each exercise offers a unique path to introspection, the key lies in consistent practice. Over time, it becomes less about doing and more about being, guiding us toward a more genuine understanding of ourselves and our authentic nature.

Real Life Examples

Throughout history, the quest for authenticity has led countless individuals on profound journeys of self-discovery. These transformative stories, rooted in the very fabric of our shared humanity, underscore the universal desire for genuine self-expression and the inherent value of living true to oneself. Let's explore some narratives of individuals who braved societal norms and expectations to find and embrace their core truth.

Mother Teresa

Born in a modest family in Skopje, Macedonia, Mother Teresa felt a call to serve God at a very young age. She chose the challenging path of aiding the poorest of the poor in the slums of Calcutta, India. While many questioned and sometimes even criticized her methods or motivations, she remained unwavering in her dedication to the destitute, the dying, and the neglected. Living authentically to her calling, she founded the Missionaries of Charity, an order that continues her mission. Her life exemplifies how staying true to one's core truth can lead to profound service and impact, even amidst challenges and criticisms.

Nelson Mandela

Nelson Mandela, the iconic anti-apartheid activist and the first black president of South Africa is a testament to the power of authentic leadership. For 27 long years, he was imprisoned for his beliefs and fight against racial segregation. Instead of harboring resentment or seeking revenge upon his release, he chose the path of reconciliation. He worked to dismantle the country's legacy of apartheid and establish multiracial elections in 1994, in which he led the ANC to victory. Mandela's journey from prisoner to president, rooted in his authentic commitment to justice and reconciliation, serves as a beacon for leaders worldwide. His life underscores the transformative power of staying true to one's beliefs and the broader vision of unity and peace, even in the face of personal sacrifice.

Through their authentic lives, these luminaries have left legacies that continue to inspire and guide countless individuals worldwide. Their stories highlight the depth of change possible when authenticity is at the core of one's actions.

Reflection

In the fast-paced modern world, filled with fleeting trends and external pressures, seeking our authentic selves can seem daunting. However, as we've explored throughout this chapter, the rewards of such a journey are immeasurable. The narratives of renowned figures, such as Mother Teresa and Nelson Mandela, coupled with various tools and detailed reflective exercises, serve as compass points, guiding us back to who we truly are as individuals.

It's human nature to want to fit in and be accepted, and often, in this quest, we put on molds that are not our own. But imagine a life where each step is in sync with the rhythm of your heart, where decisions arise from a place of genuine introspection, and where your days resonate with purpose and passion. This isn't a dream but a tangible reality for those who dare to walk the path of self-discovery.

The journey might take work. It may require confronting long-buried fears, challenging deep-seated beliefs, or swimming against popular currents. Yet, every challenge faced and every layer peeled back brings you closer to the heart of who you are. And as you inch closer, you'll find a life that's not just lived but celebrated, a life where joy isn't just occasional but a constant companion.

So, as you close this chapter, take a moment to reflect. Understand that your unique voice, passions, dreams, and truths are treasures to be discovered. Embrace them, celebrate them, and let them guide you in painting the masterpiece that is your life. The world awaits the authentic you, the unapologetic and genuine you. And in that authenticity lies a more vibrant, meaningful, and fulfilling life than you imagined.

2

SUBCONSCIOUS TOOLS FOR
TRANSFORMATION

R ecognizing our inner world can be an ongoing
effort. Even practices intended to bring peace may
unknowingly break it and reduce intimacy with God.

God stood as our constant shelter and refuge - yet sometimes
tasks and responsibilities became too overwhelming to ignore;
I became consumed by ticking items off an endless to-do list;
at these points, I became disassociated from the divine as life
became challenging to bear; neglecting His consoling company
while dealing with its inevitable ups-and-downs.

Like small garden weeds, distractions may initially seem
harmless and unworthy of attention. Still, they grow into
something much greater over time, threatening the serenity we
once held dear. It's a reminder of those months I drifted apart from
God while trying to soothe discomfort through autonomous and
unconscious means—unintentionally creating greater chaos while

creating barriers against the peace that I had so desired in the first place!

Unchecked, these weeds can quickly grow out of control, creating havoc within our spiritual landscape. And, as with gardening, it's far easier to uproot these distractions when they are still young when we can safeguard our inner peace by immersing ourselves in the presence of God; therefore, the journey back becomes a conscious act to close off access to adversary forces while protecting harmony that is meant to flourish within us.

My approach to finding peace lies in meditation upon God's scriptures and understanding who I am within His divine realms. A rhythmic inhale of "abba" becomes my gateway into this peaceful state where I embrace my Creator as my Father while forging intimate and profound ties between myself and the divine realms. In this personal dialogue with the divine, I find nourishment similar to the tender rebirth of a soul under His gentle guidance.

Transitioning from this intimate connection, I explore creative outlets using M.A.P.S. (music, art, poetry, and short films.) These serve as a channel through which my innate creativity, mirroring the image of the Creator Himself, finds expression. From these creative outlets comes profound awareness: emotions do not define us entirely—discernment becomes our guide toward realigning who we truly are as beloved children of God.

Complex Beings

Human beings are complex beings. Our thoughts, emotions, and actions result from interactions among various factors, chief among these being our mind. This chapter will explore an aspect of our psyche that's often spoken about but rarely understood in its true depth—the duality of the conscious and subconscious mind.

Imagine the human mind as an iceberg. The tip that protrudes above the water is our conscious mind—the thoughts we're aware of, the decisions we actively make, and the emotions we feel and express. It's the realm where logic reigns supreme and where our immediate perceptions of the world form. But beneath the water, occupying a vast expanse, lies the subconscious mind. This hidden depth stores memories, shapes habits, harbors beliefs, and influences our behavior in ways we might not even be aware of. It's like the backstage crew of a play, silently and efficiently ensuring everything runs smoothly, often without the audience (or, in this case, our conscious self) recognizing its critical role.

Approach this with an open heart and a curious mind. While exploring the conscious and subconscious thought processes, we may discover new insights into who we truly are as individuals, how these two parts of our mind form who we perceive ourselves to be, influence decisions we make, and either aid or hinder our quest for authenticity.

The Conscious Mind

Navigating through daily life requires a vigilant captain. In the intricate machinery of our brain, this role is assumed by the conscious mind. It's the facet we are most familiar with, the alert part, making decisions, and processing the "now."

As mentioned before, imagine the conscious mind as the tip of an iceberg visible above the water. Our immediate awareness is responsible for decision-making, logical reasoning, and daily interactions. Every task engages our conscious mind, whether choosing what to wear or deciding the best route to work. This part of our mental framework processes what's happening around us in real-time, making sense of our immediate environment.

Influence of Societal Norms

Our conscious minds are extremely vulnerable to external stimuli. Every advertisement we watch, advice we receive, or societal expectations we encounter affect our conscious thoughts. These external forces often have profound ramifications on how our behavior changes—for instance, how we greet others or react to certain events, ensuring we conform to acceptable behavior.

Our surroundings, too, almost subtly, dictate the workings of our conscious mind. Have you ever noticed how you automatically reach for an umbrella if there are dark clouds outside, even if it's not raining yet? That's your conscious mind taking cues from the environment and acting upon it.

Relying on Conscious Awareness

The conscious mind is invaluable. Its logical processing ensures we make reasoned decisions, often safeguarding us from pitfalls. Being "in the moment," helps us respond effectively to immediate challenges, ensuring our survival and safety in various situations.

However, relying solely on our conscious awareness has its limitations. Firstly, it's influenced predominantly by the present, often neglecting past experiences or future implications. It can sometimes be swayed by immediate rewards at the cost of long-term benefits.

Furthermore, our conscious mind has a limited capacity. Like a computer's RAM, it can handle only a specific number of tasks simultaneously. Overburdening can lead to stress, hasty decisions, or even burnout.

Also, by always being in the conscious "driver's seat," we might miss out on the richness of intuition, creativity, and deep-seated beliefs our subconscious offers. Balancing the inputs from the conscious and the subconscious ensures a holistic approach to life, tapping into our immediate reasoning capabilities and the deep well of experiences and emotions beneath.

The Subconscious Mind

Immerse yourselves for just a moment below the surface of our mental ocean, where lies our subconscious. Unlike the tip-of-the-iceberg consciousness we navigate with daily, the subconscious is a profound, immense reservoir holding memories, beliefs, experiences, and emotions that may not always be at the forefront of our awareness but profoundly influence who we are.

If the conscious mind is the captain at the ship's helm, the subconscious is the deep waters the ship sails upon. This part of our mind is active 24/7, working behind the scenes, even when asleep. It's where dreams are birthed, memories, both cherished and painful, are stored, and hold onto deeply held beliefs that define who we are as individuals.

Past Traumas & Beliefs

At an early age, our subconscious mind begins storing experiences within us for later recall and use. A soothing lullaby, a frightening night, the warmth of a hug, the sting of a reprimand—all find their way into this repository. Over time, these memories, especially repeated ones, form patterns and become the beliefs that guide our lives.

For instance, children frequently praised for their efforts might grow up believing that hard work yields rewards. On the other hand, someone who faces frequent criticism might harbor a deep-seated feeling of never being "good enough." Past traumas, unfortunately, etch deep marks on the subconscious. A traumatic event can influence future reactions and behavior, even if the conscious mind doesn't always recall the event. This is why specific triggers can evoke intense emotional responses out of nowhere.

The Power of the Subconscious

Given its wealth of experiences and beliefs, it is no surprise that our subconscious mind wields such significant power over us—often having an enormous effect on our reactions, behaviors, and emotions.

Have you ever experienced an unexplainable attraction or distaste for particular objects or things, like songs that instantly bring smiles or smells that transport you back years? That is your subconscious at work!

Similarly, the subconscious manages many of our automatic behaviors, like riding a bike or playing a musical instrument. Once the conscious mind has learned the task, it's handed over to the subconscious, allowing us to perform without actively thinking about each step.

While the conscious mind deserves credit for guiding us through daily life, recognizing our subconscious's incredible depth and influence is essential. Understanding and working with both allows us to navigate our life's journey with greater self-awareness and purpose.

The Symbiotic Dance

Imagine two dancers gracefully moving across a stage in perfect unison; every step, turn, and gesture complementing one another to produce an intricate and fascinating performance for their audience. That is what it's like between our conscious and subconscious minds—they balance one another delicately, interweave seamlessly, and engage in a constant interplay that mutually influences their parts of the mind.

Consciously, our minds are continually at work processing immediate experiences and making decisions based on logic and current awareness. At the same time, however, the subconscious mind plays vital roles by feeding memories, emotions, and beliefs stored over a lifetime to our conscious minds for processing.

So when we make decisions like trusting others, our conscious mind analyzes immediate information, such as their words, actions, or expressions. At the same time, our subconscious may provide additional information that influences our decisions, such as past experiences, stored emotions, or deep-rooted beliefs about trust. All these layers combine into our perception and judgment.

For example, a talented artist is reluctant to display their work. Consciously, they might attribute their hesitation to practical reasons like lack of time or the right platform. Yet, subconsciously, an early criticism of their art during childhood may have instilled a fear of judgment. This deep-seated belief might influence conscious decisions, holding them back from showcasing their talent.

Or take someone who pulls back every time they start a new venture just when things begin to progress. On the surface, they cite reasons like market conditions or external challenges. In reality, their subconscious belief is rooted in the fear of success, perhaps stemming from witnessing the burdens of success in their family.

Techniques to Harmonize the Conscious and Subconscious

While operating on different frequencies, conscious and subconscious minds can be harmonized for optimal functioning. When we consciously tap into our subconscious reservoir, we can navigate our lives with greater clarity, balance, and purpose. Here's a guide to practical techniques to help bridge the gap between these two realms, ensuring their harmonious interplay:

Mindfulness Meditation:

Regular meditation allows one to observe thoughts non-judgmentally. Over time, this practice can reveal patterns, shedding light on subconscious beliefs influencing daily decisions.

Guided Visualization:

Find a quiet space to sit or lie down. Close your eyes and take a few deep breaths. Visualize a serene landscape—perhaps a beach, forest, or mountain. Imagine yourself walking through this landscape, observing everything around you. This act of guided visualization calms the conscious mind. It allows the subconscious to surface, making it a powerful tool for introspection.

Body Scan Meditation:

Start by focusing on the top of your head, slowly moving your attention to your toes. Notice the sensations in each part of your body. This practice grounds the conscious mind in the present moment and, in doing so, makes it more receptive to insights from the subconscious.

Observation Meditation:

Sit quietly, observing your thoughts without judgment. Visualize them as clouds passing by in the sky. This practice helps distinguish between fleeting conscious thoughts and deeper subconscious patterns.

Intuitive Decision-making:

Whenever faced with a choice, take a moment to check in with your gut feeling or intuition and analyze the situation logically.

Journaling:

Writing about daily experiences, dreams, or reactions can provide insights into the subconscious mind's workings. Over time, patterns emerge, offering clues about deep-rooted beliefs.

Affirmations:

These are positive statements that can be used to reprogram negative or limiting beliefs in the subconscious. Repeating affirmations like "I am worthy of success" can slowly shift one's mindset.

Professional Therapy:

Sometimes, deeply entrenched beliefs or traumas require professional help. Therapists can use Cognitive Behavioral Therapy (CBT) or hypnotherapy to access and address the subconscious mind.

Digital Detox:

Dedicate specific times in the day when you are free from digital distractions. This gives the conscious mind a break and allows for a deeper connection with the subconscious.

Debunking Myths About Hypnosis

Hypnosis has long been shrouded in mystery and misinterpreted; nonetheless, its potential to access our subconscious minds remains undeniable and provides avenues of healing, understanding, and growth.

Myth 1:

Hypnosis is Mind Control- Contrary to popular belief, hypnosis is not about controlling someone's mind. It's a therapeutic tool where the individual enters a heightened focus and receptivity state. The person remains in control and can choose to exit the hypnotic state anytime.

Myth 2:

Only the Weak-minded can be Hypnotized- Hypnosis has nothing to do with the strength or weakness of one's mind. Most people can be hypnotized, provided they are willing and open to the experience.

Myth 3:

Hypnosis can Retrieve Accurate Memories- Hypnosis may help people recall forgotten events; however, its accuracy depends on individual experience as memories could be altered or changed under suggestion, so this method cannot guarantee accurate memory retrieval.

The Science and Art of Hypnotherapy

Hypnotherapy, the therapeutic use of hypnosis, has deep historical roots. Ancient civilizations, including the Egyptians and Greeks, used hypnosis for healing. In the modern era, its scientific basis was furthered by figures like Franz Mesmer and Dr. Milton Erickson. Methodologies vary, but most involve a hypnotic induction—guiding the individual into a deeply relaxed state. In this trance-like state, the conscious mind takes a backseat, allowing the therapist to communicate directly with the subconscious.

Hypnotherapy's advantages are numerous; it can aid in treating anxiety, phobias, substance abuse, and chronic pain; additionally, it's an invaluable way of exploring oneself by uncovering deep-seated beliefs, memories, or traumas that might otherwise remain hidden.

The Role of Dreams and Intuition

The intricate relationship between our mind's conscious and subconscious realms, dreams, and intuition emerge as powerful messengers. They offer insights, provide guidance, and serve as bridges, connecting the two worlds. Let's look further into their mysteries to uncover how they guide our journey toward discovering core truths within ourselves.

Dreams as a Bridge

As we sleep each night, our minds go on an unpredictable and sometimes puzzling voyage through dreams. Though sometimes seen as mysterious or abstract, dreams play an essential part in psychological well-being. They provide our subconscious mind an outlet to communicate messages about our fears, desires, and reflections. While the conscious mind rests, the subconscious becomes active, weaving stories from fragments of our daily lives, past experiences, and innermost feelings.

Many ancient civilizations, including the Egyptians and Greeks, regarded dreams as divine messages or prophecies. In modern times, renowned psychologists like Carl Jung and Sigmund Freud explored dreams as windows into the deeper layers of the human psyche. They believed dreams could unravel hidden conflicts, desires, and aspects of our personality.

Analyzing the Significance in Dreams

Attention to recurring symbols, themes, or emotions in our dreams can be enlightening. For example, being chased in a dream often represents feeling threatened or avoiding a situation in waking life. Flying can symbolize a desire for freedom or escape. By journaling and reflecting on dreams, we can identify patterns that hint at unresolved issues or suppressed emotions.

Additionally, dreams can also serve as a source of inspiration and creativity. Many artists, writers, and scientists have credited their dreams for breakthrough ideas. Paul McCartney's song "Yesterday" and the chemical structure of benzene discovered by August Kekulé were both inspired by dreams.

Cultivating and Trusting Intuition

Intuition, commonly called our "gut feeling," is an integral human psychology component. Our subconscious minds use intuition to process information based on past experiences, patterns, and knowledge—providing immediate guidance or insight. While logic and reasoning serve as tools of our conscious minds, intuition is the subconscious language.

One can practice mindfulness, meditation, and deep listening to cultivate a stronger intuitive sense. Spending quiet moments in reflection, being present, and tuning into one's body sensations can sharpen intuitive abilities. Trusting this intuition, even when it defies logic, often leads to decisions that resonate with our core truths.

Dreams and intuition can serve as powerful guides. They reveal new insights, showing us ways to better align ourselves with who we truly are while encouraging us to tap into the wisdom buried deep inside ourselves.

Reflection

It is truly astounding how expansive our minds are, with its intricate dance between the conscious and subconscious realms. Throughout this chapter, we explored their distinct characteristics while noting their intertwined natures. It becomes evident that while the conscious mind is our day-to-day navigator, responding to external stimuli and making logical decisions, the deep reservoir of the subconscious often holds the keys to our most profound truths, beliefs, and memories.

Imagine what could happen when these two powerful realms aren't in conflict but, instead, they work together—think of all that could come out of that collaboration! Aligning our conscious and subconscious minds opens the path toward living more enriched, authentic, and purposeful lives; understanding its depth and subtlety helps guide conscious experiences more accurately while aligning better with core values and desires.

However, understanding and reconciling both aspects of one's mind is an ongoing journey requiring patience, curiosity, and dedication. Every step brings you closer to discovering your true nature as you discover your infinite potential within yourself.

3

— · —

GUILT, SHAME, AND LIBERATION

While feeling isolated from the world, I experienced an intense feeling of separation, which caused an outpouring of unprocessed emotions to surface and overwhelm me. Quick fixes and distractions were temporary solutions, but none brought peace or resolution to my discomfort.

This feeling stemmed from a physical injury, like when I blew out a knee. At first, the isolation felt like a break, a chance to catch up on entertainment. But as time passed, I realized a deeper issue needed attention, just like having to start physical therapy. Will I be able to come back from this? Will I be able to function to full ability? It's a long road ahead. If I think too far ahead, if I question the things of the past leading up to the injury, I am robbing myself of today. I had a lot of joy playing basketball, and now I can't.

But these injuries go beyond physical traumas. Unprocessed emotional grief, stress levels, doubts, fears, and questioning can weigh heavily on the soul, causing tightness in the chest, shortness of breath, and hyper-vigilance.

Amidst all this confusion, I began to reflect on my life and the areas where I felt bound. The isolation forced me to face my vulnerabilities and recognize the need for healing. As I aged, my childhood survival state no longer served me, and my hypervigilance intensified. Realizing I needed change, I turned toward temporary remedies such as CBD oil, painkillers, or alcohol as quick means to soothe the discomfort in my life—hoping they might provide brief respite and ease my suffering temporarily.

Yet, deep down, I knew that true solace could only be found in turning to God. I wish I had turned to Him sooner, but I didn't know what I didn't know. I used to believe that I could fix everything alone and blamed myself for not being smart or resourceful enough.

In the presence of God, I found a safe haven where I could be completely authentic. Seeking His will allowed my heart to be revealed. In that vulnerability, God could work to bring about genuine healing. I carried the weight of my past, a heavy backpack of garbage that burdened me and made me feel hunched over.

But when I finally turned to God, I found relief and healing for my emotional discomfort. It was a process, but I embraced it wholeheartedly, knowing that I could face any challenge with God by my side. And so, my transformation journey began as I walked hand in hand with God, ready to face whatever came my way.

Guilt & Shame

Some feelings in the spectrum of human emotions elevate us, filling our souls with light and buoyancy. But then, some weigh us down, shackling our spirits and dimming our inner radiance. Among the heaviest of these emotional burdens are guilt and shame. Both are universal, transcending cultures, ages, and circumstances. Yet remain amongst some of the least understood or stigmatized emotions we face daily.

At their core, guilt and shame are mechanisms of self-reflection and social alignment. Over time, they've evolved as tools of self-regulation—warning us when our behavior veers from what's considered moral or the values shared among community members. But while their origin lies within protective instincts, their intensified expression can bring great distress.

This chapter aims to dive deep into the complex world of guilt and shame, exploring their roots, manifestations, and ripple effects. By understanding these emotions, I hope to offer insights to alleviate the pain they often bring and illuminate the path to healing, acceptance, and personal growth. As we journey together through this exploration, remember that every emotion, including guilt and shame, holds a lesson. Our task is to uncover, learn from, and ultimately transform it into a stepping stone towards our greater self-awareness and well-being.

Defining Guilt and Shame

Guilt and shame often coexist within human emotions, often to such an extent that distinguishing the two may become challenging. Yet understanding their differences is paramount for self-awareness and personal growth.

Guilt is our emotional reaction to any action or inaction we perceive to be wrong; this usually stems from violating either our personal moral code or society-imposed standards that we ascribe to. For instance, you might feel guilty for forgetting a dear friend's birthday or not helping a colleague when they reached out. Guilt is tethered to specific events and is often accompanied by the wish that one should have acted differently.

On the other hand, shame penetrates deeper into our psyche, reflecting our sense of worthiness and how others view us. Shame doesn't simply focus on an act or event but paints our entire self with inadequacy or unworthiness. In the earlier example, guilt says, "I forgot my friend's birthday, and that was a bad thing to do," shame laments, "I forgot their birthday; I am a bad friend." It's not just about an action; it's a stinging indictment of our very being, murmuring, "I am bad."

Both guilt and shame serve an adaptive function in society by keeping individuals aligned with social norms and personal values; however, both emotions can lead to unintended outcomes. When experienced in healthy doses, guilt can serve as a moral compass, nudging us toward personal growth. However, excessive or misplaced guilt can lead to anxiety, indecisiveness, and depression. Shame is even more corrosive, especially when it becomes chronic or deeply ingrained. It erodes self-esteem, fosters isolation, and can precipitate various mental health issues, from depression to eating disorders. Collective shame also often prevents open discussion; it inhibits reconciliation efforts after conflicts have ended, perpetuating cycles of abuse and silence.

Though these emotions may seem daunting, understanding their roots and manifestations is the first step toward healing. By differentiating between guilt and shame, we become better prepared to address their unique causes, navigate their challenges, and use them for personal transformation.

The Root Causes

The dense forests of our minds are home to many secrets. Among them are the root causes of guilt and shame, often planted early in our lives and then watered and nurtured by subsequent experiences. By understanding the genesis of these powerful emotions, we can begin to address and heal them.

Early-Life Experiences and Triggers: Childhood years can shape many aspects of our adult emotional responses. An innocent mistake punished too harshly or consistent negative reinforcement can sow the seeds of guilt and shame. For instance, spilling milk might prompt overly angry responses from their parent. Over time, such incidents can cultivate an inner narrative where the child feels that they are constantly at fault, leading to a propensity for guilt. Following persistent negative comments about a child's capabilities or appearance can embed feelings of unworthiness, giving birth to shame.

Family, Educational, and Societal Structures: Our families are our first introduction to the world, and their beliefs, values, and reactions play a pivotal role in shaping our self-worth and moral compass. Families that set rigid moral standards or have unreasonable expectations could unintentionally foster feelings of guilt or shame that lead to poor self-image or life choices later.

Educational institutions also play a part. Their structured systems of rewards and punishments may amplify such emotions in children who feel they cannot meet the standards. Furthermore, teachers using humiliation as an intimidation tactic or classmates engaging in bullying could further deepen feelings of shame for these kids.

With its ever-shifting standards of success, beauty, and morality, society constantly sends signals. Through media, literature, and social norms, society often dictates what's "acceptable" and "taboo." Those who don't fit this mold might grapple with societal-induced shame.

Insights from Psychological Studies

Research in the area of guilt and shame has provided invaluable insights. Studies have demonstrated that children as young as three show signs of shame when they think they've disappointed a caregiver, illustrating its deeply embedded presence within human psychology. Another intriguing discovery is the body's physiological response to shame. MRI scans have demonstrated that when individuals recount shameful experiences, there's increased activity in regions related to self-perception and negative emotions in the brain.

Moreover, long-term studies have indicated that unresolved guilt and shame can contribute to various psychological disorders in adulthood, from anxiety and depression to complex post-traumatic stress disorders.

By understanding these psychological components, we gain clarity into the many interacting factors that create guilt and shame, without assigning blame but instead creating awareness leading to healing and transformation.

Cultural Conditioning and Collective Shame

Every culture, no matter its traditions or values, invariably has certain behavioral norms and expectations that serve as invisible yardsticks to measure individual actions and choices. Deviations from "accepted norms" often result in guilt and shame among individual participants and communities.

The Weight of Societal Norms:

Imagine growing up in a society where collective thinking trumps individual desires. In many Asian cultures, for instance, the concept of "saving face" is paramount. Anything that deviates from the norm—an unconventional career choice, a taboo relationship, or even personal failure—can result in significant shame for the individual and their family. This collective mindset can often compel individuals to suppress their true desires and live a life that conforms to societal standards.

Religion:

Religion plays an instrumental role in shaping our perceptions of guilt and shame, such as through Christian teachings about "original sin," an inherent human flaw that may contribute to feelings of guilt for believers. Similarly, many cultural practices rooted in religious beliefs can delineate clear boundaries of "right" and "wrong," crossing these can lead to profound feelings of shame.

Confronting Deep-seated Beliefs

Challenging or even recognizing these culturally ingrained beliefs is no small feat. Individuals who dare to defy these norms sometimes face social isolation, familial alienation, or personal crises. The internal turmoil of grappling with one's beliefs, conditioned over a lifetime, versus the pull of societal expectations, can be unbearable.

However, there's a silver lining. As the world becomes more interconnected, there's a gradual broadening of perspectives. Exposure to diverse cultures and thoughts slowly reshapes many societies' rigid structures of guilt and shame. Moreover, once silenced, the voices of dissent are now finding resonance in global platforms, challenging age-old beliefs and advocating for change.

Breaking the Chains

The deeply entrenched guilt and shame can seem like unconquerable barriers to personal growth and well-being. Yet, breaking free from these emotional shackles is possible with the right tools and guidance. This journey of liberation, though challenging, is profoundly rewarding, allowing individuals to experience a renewed sense of freedom, authenticity, and self-worth.

Therapy:

Therapy, be it group, individual, or self-guided, offers a safe space to confront, process, and release feelings of guilt and shame. A trained therapist can provide insight into the root causes of these emotions and offer strategies for managing and eventually overcoming them. But many other proactive exercises can aid healing for those who aren't able or ready to take that route.

Guided Visualizations:

Visualizations can be a tool to combat guilt and shame. They involve creating mental imagery that challenges and ultimately replaces the negative beliefs associated with these emotions. For example, envisioning oneself in a situation that previously evoked shame but reacting with self-compassion and understanding instead of self-deprecation can gradually shift internal narratives.

Journaling for Insight:

Putting pen to paper has always been a time-tested method for introspection. Regularly journaling about instances that trigger feelings of guilt or shame can offer clarity on recurring patterns. Questions to ponder:

- What was the exact situation?

- How did I feel at that moment?

- Why did I feel that way?

Over time, this practice can foster a deeper understanding of triggers and help develop coping mechanisms.

Self-Forgiveness

Few experiences in human emotion are as liberating and yet challenging as self-forgiveness. Amid feelings of guilt and shame, finding self-forgiveness may offer relief and healing—yet how does one navigate this path when riddled with past regrets and harsh self-judgments?

Self-criticism can often become our own harshest critic. While infringements committed by others might easily pass unnoticed, when seen through our own evaluation lenses, they can seem far greater, create negative self-perceptions, and prevent growth altogether.

Self-forgiveness doesn't involve downplaying our mistakes and shortcomings; rather, it entails acknowledging them, learning from them, and choosing to move on with life afterward. By understanding our actions' root causes and taking responsibility, self-forgiveness allows us to view ourselves as imperfect beings on an ever-evolved journey towards personal transformation; herein lies its transformative power.

Empathy should not only be directed toward others; we must extend it toward ourselves, too. Mistakes happen to everyone, and understanding this shared frailty can foster self-compassion. By treating ourselves with the same kindness and acceptance, forgiveness becomes easier to achieve.

Recognizing the Need for a Helping Hand

Just as a ship uses a lighthouse to navigate rough waters, individuals may need therapists, counselors, or support groups to guide them through treacherous terrains of guilt and shame. But how does one know when it's time to reach out? The signs might vary—from persistent feelings of worthlessness and self-blame to heightened anxiety and depression. When these emotions impede daily functioning or feel too overwhelming to address alone, it might indicate the need for professional support.

Therapy isn't just a space to voice concerns; it's a sanctum of structured guidance. Professionals trained in the intricacies of human emotions can offer strategies, coping mechanisms, and new perspectives that might not be easily discernible otherwise. Whether it's Cognitive Behavioral Therapy focusing on reshaping negative thought patterns or psychoanalysis diving deep into early-life experiences, therapy can be a beacon of hope and clarity.

Support groups, too, offer a unique avenue of healing. In shared narratives and communal understanding, individuals often find solace in knowing they're not alone. This communal spirit can act as a buoyant force, lifting individuals from guilt and shame.

Reclaiming Your Narrative

Each thread in our lives is intricately interwoven with memories, decisions, and emotions, some heavy with guilt or shame, yet each person holds within him or herself the power to change these threads by taking charge and changing our narrative as best fits them—forging towards self-acceptance and love rather than looking back with regrets at past burdens or turning away from ourselves altogether.

Every individual is the author of their own life story. While we may not have control over past chapters filled with guilt and shame, we certainly possess the pen that writes the upcoming ones. Strategies such as reframing negative beliefs, challenging self-deprecating thoughts, and creating positive affirmations can be potent tools. By actively focusing on lessons learned rather than dwelling on past regrets, we can start crafting a narrative of growth and resilience.

The Power of Self-Acceptance

While searching for liberation, one of the most transformative practices is self-acceptance. By accepting all aspects of ourselves—our imperfections and past misdeeds included—we free ourselves of the chains of guilt and shame that keep us imprisoned. Further deepening self-love through treatment as you would treat a friend can have profound ramifications. It creates space for living a meaningful life with less baggage but more focus on present growth rather than past pains overshadowing it all the time.

By taking charge of our narrative, celebrating our journey, and nurturing self-love, we can open ourselves up to the liberation that awaits.

Reflection

In the vast landscape of human emotions, guilt, and shame stand as towering mountains, casting long shadows over our souls. They emerge from the crevices of our experiences, societal norms, and internal judgments, often becoming formidable barriers to genuine happiness and self-understanding.

Yet, the heart of this exploration wasn't just to understand these emotions but to find ways to rise above them. Through introspection, therapeutic exercises, and the embrace of external support, we've seen that liberation from these chains is not just a possibility but a promise.

At the heart of this healing journey is self-forgiveness. To forgive oneself is to acknowledge our human imperfections and understand that our worth isn't defined by past mistakes or societal judgments. It's about reclaiming our narrative and recognizing that guilt and shame are parts of our story but aren't the entirety.

For readers who have resonated with these words, know this: the journey might be challenging, but you are not alone. Across ages and cultures, individuals have grappled with these emotions, and many have found their path to liberation. You, too, have the strength and resilience to rewrite your story, to move from the shadows of guilt and shame into the illuminating light of self-acceptance.

4

NEUROPLASTICITY

When our minds experience trauma, it can feel like gazing upon a war-torn landscape desperately needing restoration. Much like roads or bike lanes in disrepair, restoring them back into operation requires work. Imagine driving a car down a road full of potholes, cracks, and debris, making driving very difficult leaving the road non-operational. Obstacles must be cleared, and the road must be fixed before the vehicle can proceed without causing further damage. The neural pathways in our brain function in a similar form. Obstacles must be cleared before its signals can continue successfully.

This transformation marks the transition from a mere trigger to a glimmer of hope. Post-Traumatic Stress Disorder (PTSD), once an oppressive force, loses its grip. It's a disorder defined by how it disrupts daily life, a constant state of fight or flight. However, the diligent process of self-discovery and healing leads to a phenomenon known as Post-Traumatic Growth (PTG).

PTG provides an avenue through which one can revisit past suffering, once crippling, yet now see it as a source of inner peace. The acronym PTSD, which once triggered relentless and unforgiving knee-jerk reactions lasting hours or even days, now invites one to discover their personal journey of Pause, Trust, Seek, Declare! (PTSD).

Remember, your brain's ability to heal is a testament to human resilience and its incredible journey from trauma to triumph.

One Remarkable Organ

Amongst all the complexity of human biology lies one remarkable organ: our brain. With billions of interwoven neurons composing its structure, the human brain controls bodily functions, stores memories, and shapes thoughts, feelings, and behavior. Yet for centuries, one belief persisted: the adult brain is rigid and unchangeable, with its structure set in stone after a certain age. Suggesting past traumas, habits, or genetic predispositions had left irreparable imprints that cannot change with experience or time.

Then enters the groundbreaking discovery of neuroplasticity. Neuroscience and brain imaging technologies have advanced tremendously, leading to a dramatic paradigm shift in our understanding of brain structure. Gone was the once-held belief of an immovable organ; evidence suggests our mind can adapt and change throughout life through "neuroplasticity," shattering previous assumptions while opening doors of possibility.

This chapter takes us on a voyage into neuroplasticity and its profound effect, from shaping neural pathways to healing from traumas to developing new habits—understanding neuroplasticity is both hopeful and transformative; it underscores human's inherent ability to learn, adapt, and recreate our destinies regardless of past experiences or age. Get ready to discover its power for yourself to create an even brighter and more satisfying future.

A Glimpse into History

Humans have embarked on an extraordinary evolutionary journey from the African savannas to the streets of modern cities. This voyage, marked by countless adaptations and refinements, has led to the marvel of neuroplasticity we observe today. Understanding this history offers insights into the brain's astounding adaptability and instills a deeper appreciation of our species' resilience.

Millions of years ago, our story began. Our ancestors faced immense survival challenges and had brains significantly different from our own; cognitive demands revolved around basic necessities like finding food, evading predators, and reproducing. Over time, they navigated their environments through experience-shaping interactions, such as using tools to expand and refine specific areas in the brain associated with hand-eye coordination and motor skills—regions associated with hand-eye coordination developed and refined further over time.

As millennia passed, our ancestors' environments underwent a significant transition. Each ecosystem provided its challenges, from dense forests to expansive grasslands—hunting in the wilderness and cultivating crops were required depending on where people lived. With each new skill learned or difficulty experienced came brain structure and function changes as they continuously adapted due to neuroplasticity—something essential to their survival and success as time progressed.

As complex societies developed, their cognitive demands increased significantly. Communication, social dynamics, trade, and innovation all became crucial aspects of daily life; consequently, our brain responded by expanding and refining its networks to accommodate for these stimuli—written language reinforced areas involved with visual processing and symbolic interpretation while complex social relationships added stimulation for empathy, morality, and abstract thought regions in our brains.

Today, in our technologically driven world, the brain faces yet another set of unique challenges and stimuli. From processing vast volumes of digital information to mastering intricate abilities in different domains, modern experiences continue to shape the neural landscape - evidence of its immense adaptability.

Neuroplasticity has been the silent force at every twist and turn of our species' history, ensuring our survival, growth, and progress. Recognizing this history underscores a profound truth—change and adaptability are inherent components of our identity. And as we march forward into an uncertain future, we do so with the assurance that our brains, with their boundless plasticity, are well-equipped to navigate the challenges ahead.

The Science Behind the Magic

From the pulsating neurons in a baby's brain to the deeply etched pathways in an elder's, the brain's remarkable adaptability is nothing short of magical. But like all great magic, there's a science underpinning it. This science, which challenges many traditional beliefs about our brain, is called neuroplasticity.

The word 'neuroplasticity' is derived from 'neuron,' the nerve cells in our brain, and 'plastic,' which denotes malleability. Neuroplasticity is the brain's innate ability to reorganize by forming new neural connections. Contrary to once-popular belief, our brain isn't a rigid organ with a set structure. Instead, it is a dynamic entity, continually reshaping itself in response to positive and negative experiences.

One of the most profound revelations of neuroplasticity is that it defies age constraints. Earlier theories believed that the brain's plasticity peaked during childhood and declined as we aged, implying that children were better learners than adults. While it's true that certain learning forms, like language acquisition, are more effortless during youth, research now shows that the adult brain retains a robust ability to change. Whether it's seniors picking up new hobbies or stroke patients relearning basic functions, the wonders of neuroplasticity shine through.

Over the years, numerous myths have been associated with the brain's functioning. Phrases like "we only use 10% of our brain," or the idea that brain damage is always irreversible have infiltrated popular culture. Yet, the study of neuroplasticity disproves many such misconceptions. Our brains are always active, constantly evolving, and have an astounding capacity for recovery and growth.

Neuroplasticity allows us to unlock the enormous power of human thought. No longer confined by outdated conceptions of rigidity, we stand empowered with the knowledge that we have control over molding our brains and changing the trajectory of our lives.

Understanding Neural Pathways

At the core of our brain lies an impressive network of roads, highways, and alleys called neural pathways. These are the very routes our thoughts, actions, memories, and emotions travel. Just like a path in a forest becomes more pronounced and easier to walk upon with consistent usage, our neural pathways, too, become stronger and more efficient with repeated use.

A neural pathway is a series of interconnected neurons that activate when a specific task is performed, or a particular thought arises. For instance, if you've ever driven a car or ridden a bicycle, you might recall the initial challenges of coordinating your movements. But over time, as you practiced, it became almost second nature. This shift from requiring more effort to less effort is due to the strengthening of neural pathways associated with that activity.

One of the guiding principles underlying neural pathways is "neurons that fire together, wire together." This concept highlights repetition's power; when an action or thought is repeated over an extended period, its associated neural pathway becomes stronger; by contrast, when activation for that pathway decreases due to inactivity over an extended time, its strength begins ebbing away as per "use it or lose it."

Repetition plays a crucial role in habit formation. Habits, whether biting our nails, smoking, or exercising regularly, result from strengthened neural pathways. When we perform an action consistently, the brain recognizes the pattern. It streamlines the process, making it more efficient and automatic.

So, can old habits ever truly die? Fortunately, with the brain's plasticity, the answer is a resounding "yes." While strong neural pathways, especially those formed over decades, can be resilient, they aren't invincible. The key to "unlearning" an old habit or forming a new one lies in creating a new neural pathway and strengthening it through consistent repetition while simultaneously allowing the old pathway to weaken by not activating it.

Understanding this dynamic is empowering. It means that no habit is set in stone. We can steer our brains towards new learnings and behaviors with conscious effort, patience, and persistence. It's like forging a new path in a dense forest; initially, it requires effort and deliberate intent, but over time, as we walk that path repeatedly, it becomes more accessible and evident.

To harness the power of neural pathways in personal growth:

1. **Awareness:** Recognize the habits or thought patterns you wish to change.

2. **Intention:** Set a clear goal. What new habit or thought pattern would you like to cultivate?

3. **Consistency:** Repeatedly engage in the desired action or thought. The more you practice, the stronger the associated neural pathway becomes.

4. **Patience:** Understand that weakening an old pathway and strengthening a new one is a process. Celebrate small victories along the way.

5. **Reinforcement:** Use positive reinforcement, like rewards or affirmations, to encourage the desired behavior.

Harnessing the Brain's Potential

Neuroplasticity provides an exciting prospect: our brain can change throughout life in incredible and complex ways that may seem almost miraculous to us, not merely as passive traits but actively used for personal growth, overcoming obstacles, or healing from past traumas. By understanding how best to utilize this remarkable property of our minds, we become master sculptors ourselves!

A critical aspect of promoting positive neuroplasticity is intentionality. It's not about random experiences but targeted and purposeful interventions that can help carve out the desired neural patterns. One of the most potent tools at our disposal is mindfulness. Rooted in ancient practices but validated by modern science, mindfulness emphasizes being present in the moment observing thoughts and feelings without judgment. This attentive state has been shown to foster neuroplastic changes, enhancing brain areas linked with awareness, empathy, and emotional regulation. Meditation, a structured form of mindfulness, also holds immense potential. Regular meditation sessions can lead to many neural changes, including strengthening the prefrontal cortex, which plays a crucial role in decision-making, planning, and self-control.

Targeted cognitive and physical exercises can also play a pivotal role in reshaping our brains. Whether engaging in new learning, taking up a novel hobby, or even incorporating specific brain-training apps, these activities challenge and stretch our neural capacities, forming new connections and pathways. Physical activities, especially those that require coordination, like dancing or martial arts, also promote neuroplasticity by forcing the brain to adapt and learn continuously.

Neuroplasticity offers great promise but also poses its share of obstacles and difficulties. Resistance, setbacks, and old habits may initially seem impossible. Still, it should instead be seen as part of the journey, providing opportunities to adapt, grow, and overcome them, further solidifying its plastic nature.

Guided Exercises for Positive Neural Pathways

Here are some guided exercises designed to facilitate the creation and reinforcement of beneficial neural pathways.

Breath Focus Meditation

- Objective: To enhance focus attention and regulate the brain's emotional center.

- Procedure

  - Sit comfortably in a quiet place, closing your eyes.

  - Begin by taking deep, deliberate breaths.

  - As you breathe in, count to four, hold for a count of four, and exhale for a count of four.

  - If your mind wanders, gently bring it back to the breath without judgment.

  - Continue for 5-10 minutes daily, gradually increasing the duration as you become more accustomed.

Neurobics: Brain Aerobics

- Objective: To stimulate the brain by introducing new experiences and breaking routine patterns.

- Procedure:

  - Change a daily routine, like brushing your teeth with your non-dominant hand.

  - Take a different route to work or while running errands.

  - Blindfold yourself and try to identify objects in a room using only touch and smell.

Progressive Visualization

- Objective: To enhance creativity and visualization skills and stimulate the brain's right hemisphere.

- Procedure:

  - Close your eyes and imagine a serene place, like a beach or a forest.

  - Progressively add details to the scene: the sound of waves, the feel of sand under your feet, the warmth of the sun.

  - Dive deeper by visualizing interactions in that environment: building a sandcastle, talking to a forest creature, etc.

Memory Strengthening Game

- Objective: To improve memory and stimulate the hippocampus, the brain's memory center.

- Procedure:

  ○ Start by memorizing a list of 5 unrelated items.

  ○ Recite them, try to recall after an hour, and then again after 24 hours.

  ○ Gradually increase the list's length and complexity as your memory muscle strengthens.

Problem-Solving Challenges

- Objective: To strengthen logical thinking and decision-making and stimulate the prefrontal cortex.

- Procedure:

  ○ Engage in puzzles, brainteasers, or strategy games.

- Reflect on personal challenges and brainstorm multiple solutions, weighing the pros and cons.

Consistency is key when it comes to harnessing the power of neuroplasticity! While these exercises might seem simple, their repeated practice can profoundly affect the brain's structure and function. The aim is not to overwhelm oneself but to integrate these activities into daily life, making them as routine as brushing one's teeth. Over time, as beneficial neural pathways become reinforced more regularly, the brain becomes better at skills like focus, creativity, and problem-solving.

Limitations of Neuroplasticity

While neuroplasticity reveals that the brain can adapt, change, and heal itself, it's important to recognize that it is not a solution for all cognitive or neural challenges. For instance, severe brain injuries might lead to permanent deficits, and neuroplasticity alone may not reverse such damage. Moreover, some conditions, like advanced neurodegenerative diseases, can limit the extent of the brain's ability to rewire itself.

Another point of consideration is the age factor. Although neuroplasticity occurs throughout life, its extent and nature can differ across age groups. For instance, young brains are often more malleable, making language acquisition or learning an instrument more seamless in childhood. However, adults can still learn new skills; it might just require more time and consistent effort.

Be mindful of potential obstacles on the journey towards harnessing brain adaptability. Not all changes to the brain are beneficial—repeated exposure to stress, trauma, or negative experiences may create neural pathways that might not serve your best interest. Thus reinforcing how important positive experiences are in developing the adaptable mind. Misunderstandings about neuroplasticity are numerous, thanks to our increasingly connected world. For instance, one might come across exaggerated claims regarding "brain-boosting" exercises or supplements promising to enhance neuroplasticity—it is wise to approach such claims with suspicion and seek evidence-based information when making such claims.

Reflection

Life is an ongoing cycle of growth and evolution. By exploring neuroplasticity's intricate workings, it has become evident that our minds play an active role in molding experiences rather than passively receiving them; this realization highlights the potential hidden inside our intricate neural landscape.

It's fascinating to think that every thought we entertain, every challenge we face, and every new skill we acquire can reshape our brains. This understanding illuminates the resilience of the human spirit and the boundless capacity for renewal and reinvention in each of us.

With knowledge comes great responsibility: now that we understand how easily our brain adapts, the responsibility falls on us to create meaningful experiences, nurture healthy habits, and foster an environment conducive to personal development.

It is time to stop complacency and actively participate in neural rewiring processes!

Adopting neuroplasticity principles goes well beyond academic interest: it is about carving the path toward a fulfilling and richer existence without being limited by past experiences or outdated beliefs. Every moment offers us an opportunity to shape our brains, redefine our story, and discover more of ourselves while reaching for greater heights of accomplishment.

So now is the time; with insights and possibilities at our disposal, the invitation becomes clear: pledge yourself as lifelong learners and remain perpetually curious. In harnessing brain potential, we not only optimize neural pathways; instead, we create meaning in our lives!

— • —

FEEL TO HEAL

When you let yourself FEEL
You can let yourself HEAL
Old motivations REVEALED
Like drawn weapons CONCEALED.

This shame, You give GRACE
My past worries ERASED
An old heart, You REPLACED
Prodigal homies EMBRACED.

Arrived on scene, just as I WAS
Was fearful then, but never JUDGED.
Not incomplete, you said "I'm ENOUGH,
My yoke is chill, My Love is TOUGH.

I paid the cost, nailed on that CROSS
Blood shining bright, like MAC lip GLOSS.
You bring me joy, but I ain't your BOSS
FULL compensation, no taxes LOST.

He got me covered, no turning BACK
Armored and strapped, no things I LACK
Old ways is gone, my squad is STACKED
Blindside with mercy, new QuarterBACKS.

I fumbled daily, now less and LESS
Ran out of breath, like full court PRESS
Option to pray, or practice STRESS
I'm on the team, my greatest FLEX.

Like forming clay, babies in WOMBS
You play no games, no looney TUNES
Like butterflies, stuck in COCOONS
You'll raise me high, like "UP" BALLOONS.

Transformation

5

—— • ——

BREATHWORK & STILLNESS

A t an unexpected point on my transformation journey, I discovered a method - that promised more than it initially revealed. It was breathwork. It transcends its physical act of inhaling and exhaling; it engages one with one's subconscious while offering transformation through breath.

At first, this concept seemed simple, yet its implications were profound: our bodies hold unspoken scores of pain and grief that form an invisible record within our tissues. Therefore, I ventured on this breathwork journey with curiosity and caution, aware that what lay below could be both profoundly amazing and equally troubling.

As I dived deeper into my meditation and breathing practices, I realized that breathing wasn't just a necessary act that we do unconsciously. But, it could act as a portal into the innermost parts of our minds. It holds the key to unlocking and releasing our emotional baggage, often from the deepest parts of our subconscious.

Breathing was conscious and subconscious in equal parts; its power could tap into the vagus nerve to soothe the sympathetic nervous system and invite the body to express what lay hidden beneath the layers of consciousness.

Working in the hospital, where my daily mission was to help people breathe, I couldn't help but draw the similarities. Within our physiology's intricate web existed something like a biological conductor—an electrical current delivered by the nerve within the diaphragm. This current signals our brains, urging us to inhale and exhale, often without conscious awareness.

With intentional and focused breathwork, we could take control of the subconscious and steer it consciously toward our deeper selves. By controlling how and where our breath goes, we can move its flow deep within.

It was during one such breathwork session that I had an extraordinary experience. As I breathed, each inhale and exhale seemed to peel back the layers of time, transporting me to a moment before memory, to the warmth and safety of the womb. There, I confronted the primal fear of separation from my parents, a fear that had unknowingly shaped my existence.

But this time, there was no fear. In the embrace of breathwork, I could return to that vulnerable moment and cradle my baby self in reassurance. I whispered, "I am good, it's okay," and for the first time, the fear went away. I was at peace.

This profound encounter with my past was a turning point on my path to authenticity. It allowed me to reach higher emotional frequencies, removing the weight of unprocessed trauma and fear.

It was a transformational journey that brought me to a place of profound gratitude.

Now, I share this testimony to the world with sincerity, humility and authenticity. It's not about ego; it's about the power of authenticity. This is me—a living testament to the alchemy of breathwork. This practice goes beyond respiratory therapy, by guiding us to the deepest layers of our existence.

Ancient Origins of Breathwork

Breathing, seemingly an effortless action, has long been used as part of spiritual and healing traditions worldwide. The universal nature of ancient practices attests to its profound importance for human experience.

Over a thousand years ago, in the heart of India, sages and yogis discovered and harnessed the power of breathing through "pranayama." The Sanskrit word "prana" means vital life force, and "ayama" means to extend or draw out. Thus, pranayama can be translated as the "extension of life force" or "mastery over breath." These practices were not mere respiratory exercises but tools to navigate one's inner universe, harmonize the energies within and attain elevated states of consciousness.

Let us take a look at the indigenous cultures of the Americas. Shamanic practices held breathing in deep reverence. Breathing was the wind of the spirit, a conduit for healing energy, and a bridge to the ancestral realm. Shamans tapped into altered states of consciousness through altered breathing patterns during ceremonies, seeking guidance, visions, or insights for healing and community well-being.

Furthermore, in ancient Chinese traditions, "Qi" or "Chi," the vital energy flowing within all living beings, could be cultivated and balanced through 'Qigong' breathing techniques. By mastering one's Qi, individuals could promote healing, longevity, and spiritual awakening.

In their meditative practices, Buddhist monks also emphasized the importance of breathing. Mindful breathing became a path to enlightenment, a way to be present in the moment, and a tool to cultivate compassion and understanding.

Regardless of their geographical and cultural differences, these varied practices share a unifying truth: breathing can be an avenue between our physical realities and intangible dimensions of spirituality and consciousness. Breathwork is never simply about inhaling oxygen or exhaling carbon dioxide; instead, it's a journey toward self-discovery, healing, and communion with the divine.

Breathwork in the Modern Age

In today's fast-paced world, where technology and science dominate much of our understanding, breathwork has seen renewed attention in our modern world of technology and science. As more individuals deal with the stresses and anxieties of modern life, turning inwards and harnessing the power of breathing offers hope for relief and balance.

Recent decades have witnessed an ever-increasing fascination with breathwork's physiological and psychological benefits, with scientific research beginning to confirm what ancient cultures knew instinctively: controlled breathing can significantly influence our well-being. Studies using functional magnetic resonance imaging (fMRI) and other technologies have highlighted how certain breathing techniques activate the parasympathetic nervous system known as "rest and digest," leading to reduced stress levels, lower blood pressure levels, and enhanced feelings of relaxation and calmness.

Research demonstrates the efficacy of intentional breathing to regulate our emotions, making us better equipped to face emotional challenges with greater control. Furthermore, intentional breathing can aid against anxiety disorders, post-traumatic stress disorder, and depression.

Similar to this scientific exploration, the modern age has seen an upsurge in contemporary breathwork techniques. Holotropic Breathwork, founded by Dr. Stanislav Grof in the late 20th century, is one such technique that uses breathing patterns to induce altered states of consciousness for self-exploration and healing. Similarly, the Wim Hof Method, named after its Dutch founder, combines specific breathing techniques with cold exposure and meditation to enhance physical and mental performance, boost the immune system, and foster a sense of empowerment.

Incorporating these techniques, holistic health practitioners and wellness centers worldwide integrate breathwork into their offerings, recognizing its transformative potential. These sessions often combine the spiritual dimensions of breathwork, emphasizing intention and presence, with the science-backed physiological benefits.

Stillness

Stillness often implies stagnation or laziness; however, true stillness should not be confused with non-movement; rather, it represents an intense state of being that invites introspection, clarity, and peace into one's being.

Stillness transcends the physical realm. While stillness may manifest as physical inactivity, its essence lies deeper. Philosophically speaking, stillness resembles an undisturbed lake or pond reflecting reality without distortion; stillness is the grounding force that keeps all activity moving forward smoothly and effortlessly. It serves as the eye of the storm around which all activities revolve.

Spiritually, many traditions hold stillness in high regard. Buddhist practices emphasize the value of quietening one's mind to more clearly perceive reality without illusions; Christian contemplatives refer to "prayer of quiet" wherein one soaks up God without needing words; Taoism recognizes stillness as its natural state—which does not indicate lack of activity but rather action taken harmoniously with it.

Psychologically, stillness offers rest from the continuous chatter of our minds. It provides a sanctuary where we can disengage from the grip of anxieties, fears, and the relentless drive for achievement. In embracing stillness, the mind finds space to process, rejuvenate, and gain clarity, which can lead to more purposeful action.

Chill and Be Still

Breathwork and stillness, alone, each offer profound benefits, but together, they create a potent synergy that can create deep inner transformations.

The act of conscious breathing roots us firmly in the present moment. Each inhalation and exhalation become anchors, keeping us grounded among the swirling currents of thoughts, emotions, and external distractions. Each breath bridges the conscious and unconscious mind between the seen and the unseen realms of our existence. When harnessed with intention, it becomes a powerful tool for healing and bringing discernment.

Stillness, on the other hand, provides the canvas for revelations. Without external stimulation, your mind turns inward, diving deep into its layers. Once noise from outside has subsided, whispers from within become audible.

Transformation can come quickly through the collaboration of these two. Individuals often report experiencing greater self-awareness, uncovering deep-buried emotions, and experiencing a connection to something greater than themselves. Moments of clarity arise that provide solutions to previously insurmountable challenges or unveil hidden life paths.

So, how can one embark on this inward journey and cultivate a daily habit of stillness combined with deep breathing?

1. **Set a Dedicated Time:** Consistency is key, like any other practice. Dedicate a specific time each day, even if it's just for a few minutes initially, to sit in stillness and focus on your breath.

2. **Create a Relaxful Environment:** Find a quiet space where you won't be disturbed. Dim the lights, light a candle or incense, and play soft, ambient music.

3. **Use Guided Techniques:** There are plenty of techniques to guide one into deep breathing and stillness. One popular method is the "4-7-8 technique," where you inhale for 4 counts, hold for 7, and exhale for 8. As you get comfortable, you can explore more advanced techniques.

4. **Stay Patient and Open:** Getting distracted or restless is natural, especially when starting. Gently bring your focus back to your breath without judgment. Over time, the intervals of true stillness will increase.

5. **Integrate Micro-Moments:** Apart from a dedicated practice, find "micro-moments" throughout the day to breathe deeply and be still, even if just for a few breaths.

Guided Breathing Sessions

Here are some detailed guided breathing sessions tailored for people at different stages:

For Beginners: The Calming Breath

Objective: Reduce anxiety, calm the mind, and ground oneself in the present moment.

1. **Position:** Sit comfortably with your spine erect on a chair or cross-legged on the floor. Rest your hands on your lap. Close your eyes.

2. **Technique:** Inhale deeply through your nose for a count of 4. Hold your breath for a count of 4. Exhale slowly through your nose for a count of 6.

3. **Duration:** Repeat this cycle for 5 minutes.

Tip: Visualize a serene place, such as a quiet beach or a tranquil forest, as you breathe.

Caution: If you feel lightheaded, return to your normal breathing pattern.

For Intermediates: The Energizing Breath

Objective: Boost mental alertness, increase energy levels, and invigorate the body.

1. **Position:** Sit or stand with your spine straight. Open your eyes or keep them closed, as per your preference.

2. **Technique:** Inhale rapidly through your nose for a count of 2, followed by a rapid exhale for a count of 2. This is like a "sniffing" action.

3. **Duration:** Continue this pattern for 1 minute, then take a few deep, slow breaths and relax. You can repeat this cycle 2-3 times.

Tip: This technique can be beneficial during mid-day slumps or before mentally demanding tasks.

Caution: Avoid practicing if you feel dizzy or if rapid breathing feels uncomfortable.

For the Advanced: The 4-7-8 Breath

Objective: Improve concentration, promote relaxation, and aid in sleep.

1. **Position:** Lie down comfortably. Place one hand on your abdomen and the other on your chest.

2. **Technique:** Close your eyes and exhale completely through your mouth, making a whoosh sound. Close your mouth and inhale quietly through your nose for a count of 4. Hold your breath for a count of 7. Exhale completely through your mouth, making a whoosh sound for a count of 8.

3. **Duration:** Complete this cycle for four breaths. You can extend it up to eight breaths as you become more experienced.

Tip: This technique can be particularly effective before sleep or during high stress.

Caution: Ensure you're in a safe environment, especially if practicing before sleep, to avoid falling asleep abruptly.

Reflection

Breathwork and stillness are more than just practices; they are gateways to our innermost selves, offering paths to clarity, peace, and profound understanding. Rooted in ancient wisdom, these practices have transcended cultural boundaries and stood the test of time, resonating with generation after generation. And it's not hard to see why. As the world around us accelerates, a moment of pure, undistracted silence and rhythmic breathing becomes even more important.

In our modern age of hustle and distractions, losing touch with ourselves is easy. We often find ourselves feeling scattered, overwhelmed, and disconnected. This is where the magic of breathwork and intentional stillness comes in. By grounding us in the present moment, these practices invite a return to simplicity, reminding us of the power that resides within. The ability to calm a racing mind, to heal from within, and to connect with a more profound sense of purpose.

But more than just individual benefits, breathwork and stillness are universal languages, bridging gaps between people, cultures, and philosophies. They offer a shared experience, a collective sigh of relief in a world that sometimes feels chaotic. They remind us that beneath the surface-level differences, our hearts beat in unison while sharing breath rhythmically.

As we reflect on the profound nature of these practices, there's a powerful message for all of us. A call to slow down, to breathe deeply, and to cherish moments of stillness. It's an invitation to prioritize our mental, emotional, and spiritual well-being, recognizing that a world of discoveries is waiting in the inhalation and exhalation.

Let this encourage you: the transformative journey of breathwork and stillness awaits you! Take this journey within to discover more of yourself as the world continues to spin; may you find comfort, tranquility, and a deeper understanding of life itself.

6

— · —

TIMELINE THERAPY

In life's darkest times, it is often said that every soul wants a witness, someone who acknowledges their struggle and can validate the depths of their pain. During one of the most trying periods of my life, I felt the world changing around me. It wasn't the same lens through which I had once looked upon life. The colors seemed different, the air heavier.

"Why is this happening to me?" was a question that echoed repeatedly within the chambers of my heart. Like many during those testing times, I found comfort in the narrative of victimhood. It wasn't a choice; it felt like the only mode of survival. During this, gaslighting, the sinister tool used by narcissists, cast me into a spiral of self-doubt, making me examine my every move while they danced around their responsibilities. Furthermore, gaslighting from narcissists caused further self-doubt, making me question my every move while they avoided taking responsibility.

With a past tainted by unresolved childhood trauma and a tendency to please others, I lost my cherished dialogue with the Divine. I clung to relationships, seeking harmony even where it felt distant, especially with my parents. It was a time of personal revival. I took stands that resonated with my spirit, even if it was hard for the world to understand. Today, I can see my mistakes with wisdom, but back then, I was a sailor in stormy seas with only a dim lantern to guide me.

The journey towards inner transformation often begins with silence—a moment when one listens to the noise within. How many of those shouts and whispers in our minds speak the truth? And how many are shadows of deceit? Back then, the weight of grief, the sharp sting of fear, and the looming shadow of self-preservation clouded my vision.

The clouds began to lift in January 2022 when I was christened with a name for my pain: Post Traumatic Stress Disorder (PTSD). What was PTSD for me? A 'moral injury,' a wound that didn't bleed but was etched deep within my spirit. And just like any scar, it needed its time to heal.

Then, as winter came to a close, a new chapter began on February 26, 2022, the birth of our son, Myles. Although new life surrounded me, old habits clung on. I continued to anesthetize my pain until one defining moment when I decided: I am effin' done suffering! This resolution led me to the doors of Save a Warrior, a beacon in my storm.

The road ahead was challenging. Facing the looming giants of alcohol, pain killers, and marijuana, I knew their allure could easily become my downfall. Yet, in this hour of despair, I felt divine intervention. "BUT GOD!" It was as if God, leaving the 99, came searching for me, pulling me from the depths of the Earth.

With surrender came renewal. Every challenge and hurdle I faced was a testament to my resilience. I was alive, surrounded by love, sheltered in a new house. All I needed was to lean on faith, one day at a time.

God had a revelation for me: the scars of my past, which once shielded me, were now chains. It was time to break free. So, shedding prejudices, I turned to medical aid for ADHD, anxiety, and PTSD. With every pill, the world's relentless pace seemed to ease. Coupled with meditation and prayers, I found an oasis of calm where God's whispers reached me.

And so, through the rubble of trauma and pain, I emerged—stronger, clearer, and more connected to God than ever before.

Timeline Therapy

Timeline Therapy (TLT) stands out among therapeutic approaches as an innovative technique that goes deep into our subconscious to untangle emotional traumas. TLT was not created out of thin air; instead, it arose from understanding human behavior, language usage patterns, and how memory forms within us.

Its origins are firmly rooted in neuro-linguistic programming (NLP). This groundbreaking approach highlights the relationship between language, thoughts, and behavior patterns. NLP provided a foundation upon which TLT was built, offering tools and perspectives that form the bedrock of TLT's methodologies.

Yet, Timeline Therapy offers something distinct. While NLP focuses on the interplay of language and thought, TLT goes further by going on a temporal journey. It operates on the belief that our past, present, and future are linked in a continuum, and by navigating this timeline, we can address and heal emotional wounds that may have been buried or overlooked.

TLT allows individuals to revisit, reassess, and reframe pivotal moments. This therapy does not skim the surface but addresses the very root of emotional traumas, offering a unique pathway to healing and transformation. We will venture further into Timeline Therapy, uncovering its nuances, methodologies, and profound impact on the human mind.

The Philosophy of Timeline Therapy

At its heart, TLT doesn't just explore the 'what' and 'why' of our experiences; it dives into the 'when.' This distinction is pivotal in understanding the transformative power of TLT.

The foundational idea of TLT lies in the belief that we all possess an internal "timeline" that chronicles our life's journey. It's not a chronological record but a reservoir where memories, emotions, beliefs, and decisions are stored and connected. Picture a large piece of fabric, with threads representing different moments of our lives, colored by the emotions we felt at those times. These distinct threads are woven, influencing our present selves and shaping our future paths.

However, it's essential to recognize that this timeline isn't just a storage system. Instead, it continually evolves and shifts based on new experiences and insights. This understanding forms the backbone of TLT's therapeutic approach, allowing practitioners to navigate an individual's timeline, accessing memories and emotions that may hold the key to current challenges or limiting beliefs.

By revisiting past experiences, TLT provides us with a powerful opportunity to reframe and resolve these memories in new ways. Imagine holding onto an old photograph as you view it through new eyes; understand its context more fully and give it a new frame that changes its essence altogether—that's the power TLT offers: instead of being trapped down with past traumas or negative emotions, individuals become empowered to revisit these moments from different viewpoints, understanding them with fresh eyes yet altering the emotional charge associated with each moment.

But why does reframing matter so much? Our past experiences, particularly those that stir strong emotions, often become scripts we use when making decisions and acting out behaviors. By altering the narrative or emotional weight of past events through TLT therapy, individuals gain freedom from these scripts to move forward freely without burden.

Timeline Therapy is more than a therapeutic approach; it's a philosophical lens that challenges our perceptions of time, memories, and healing. By bridging the past, present, and future,

TLT offers a holistic pathway to self-discovery, empowerment, and transformation.

How it Works

Timeline Therapy (TLT) is not just a theoretical concept—it is an actual structured process designed to bring about genuine change. To appreciate its potency fully, it's necessary to fully grasp its mechanisms and systemic approach.

A pivotal player in this process is the subconscious mind. While our conscious mind engages with the immediate, the here and now, our subconscious mind is the guardian of our memories, beliefs, and long-held emotions. It's the reservoir that TLT taps into. Why? Because within the realms of our subconscious lie answers to many of our current challenges. TLT operates on the premise that we can be guided to transformational change by accessing, understanding, and modifying these subconscious memories and beliefs.

To explore the subconscious mind, TLT employs many techniques, many rooted in neuro-linguistic programming (NLP). Through guided visualization, specific questioning, and other methods, practitioners help individuals trace back to the root cause of their issues. Once these root events are identified, TLT offers techniques to detach the negative emotions or limiting beliefs associated with them. It's like defusing a time bomb, where the explosive charge (negative emotion or belief) is safely removed, rendering the bomb (past memory) harmless.

However, TLT isn't an island in the vast ocean of therapeutic interventions. Its relationship with other forms of therapy is complementary. While TLT specifically addresses the temporal aspect of memories and emotions, other therapeutic methods might look into the content or nature of these experiences. Integrating TLT with other interventions offers a multi-dimensional healing approach, addressing issues from various angles.

In summary, Timeline Therapy is a systematic journey into the subconscious mind, seeking to reframe and resolve past traumas and negative emotions. Interacting seamlessly with other therapeutic methods provides a comprehensive tool for healing and personal growth, anchored in the understanding that our past, while influential, doesn't have to dictate our future.

Practical Sessions

Timeline Therapy (TLT) is more than just a therapeutic method – it's a journey across one's personal timeline, from past wounds to future aspirations. Like any journey, embarking on TLT requires preparation, guidance, and a clear map. Here's how the therapeutic journey unfolds in practice:

Setting the Stage: A TLT session begins by selecting the right intentions. Before venturing into the depths of the subconscious, it's crucial to establish a safe and supportive environment. The practitioner and the individual work collaboratively to define the session's goals, ensuring that both are aligned in purpose. The primary objective is to create a therapeutic space built on mutual trust and respect, ensuring the individual feels secure and ready to go into their memories.

Embarking on the journey: With the foundation set, the exploration begins. Using specialized techniques, the practitioner guides the individual through their internal timeline. This could involve revisiting past memories, understanding current beliefs, or even visualizing potential future events. Each stage serves a purpose: past memories often hold the roots of current challenges, present beliefs dictate current behaviors and envisioned future events can inspire change and growth.

Transforming Emotions and Beliefs: A significant portion of TLT involves identifying and changing negative emotions or beliefs. As one travels back to crucial events, one may encounter memories filled with anger, sadness, fear, hurt, or guilt. If left unchecked, these stored emotions can have cascading effects on present-day life. TLT offers techniques to confront these emotions head-on, allowing individuals to release their grip and find a resolution. The process isn't about erasing memories but transforming the emotional charge they carry.

Integrating the Positive: Releasing negative emotions and limiting beliefs creates a vacuum that TLT aims to fill with positive, empowering emotions and beliefs. Positive anchoring allows individuals to visualize and internalize empowering feelings and perspectives. This ensures that past wounds are healed, and the path ahead is illuminated with hope and purpose.

Continued Practice: Like any therapy, the effectiveness of TLT increases with repetition and continued practice. Over time, individuals learn to naturally navigate their internal timelines, using the tools and techniques from their sessions to face life's challenges with resilience and clarity.

Addressing Skepticism and Concerns

The realm of psychotherapy is varied, with numerous modalities claiming relief, resolution, and insight. Among these, Timeline Therapy (TLT) stands out for its unique approach and the skepticism it occasionally invites. To fully appreciate its potential, addressing the misconceptions and concerns surrounding TLT is important.

One common concern is the fear of 'tampering' with memories. Some worry that revisiting traumatic past events might alter or distort their recollection of the past. However, seasoned practitioners emphasize that TLT isn't about changing the memory itself but rather the emotional charge associated with it. The objective is to detach the negative emotions or limiting beliefs from the event, allowing the individual to view their past through a lens of understanding and empowerment.

Another frequent misconception is the idea that TLT might be a quick fix. The belief that one can simply 'time travel' and eradicate years of pain and conditioning in a single session is a misrepresentation. While many individuals report significant shifts even after one session, the therapy's depth and effectiveness often rely on continued introspection and application. It's a journey, and like any other therapeutic process, its success is influenced by the individual's commitment and the therapist's skill.

Safety is a legitimate concern, especially when dealing with traumatic memories. Some critics argue that bringing up traumatic events without proper support can be retraumatizing. This is where the expertise of the practitioner becomes paramount. A qualified TLT therapist is trained to create a safe space, ensuring the individual feels supported and grounded. Moreover, suppose a particular memory is too painful to revisit. In that case, a skilled practitioner will use techniques that allow healing without direct confrontation.

Lastly, there's the criticism that TLT is just a repackaged version of other therapeutic modalities, particularly given its roots in neuro-linguistic programming (NLP). While TLT does draw from NLP techniques, it has its distinct methodology, focusing explicitly on the chronological sequencing of memories and emotions.

To debunk myths and misconceptions about TLT, one must turn to empirical evidence, expert opinions, and, most importantly, the countless testimonials of those who've undergone the therapy. When practiced under qualified guidance, TLT offers a unique path to healing, allowing individuals to reframe their past, reshape their present, and envision a more positive future.

Preparing for a Timeline Therapy Session

Beginning a Timeline Therapy (TLT) journey is a significant decision, often driven by a desire for profound healing and self-awareness. However, like any therapeutic process, the outcomes of TLT are influenced not only by the methodology itself but also by the individual's preparedness and the therapist's expertise. With that in mind, here are some essential considerations for those contemplating TLT.

Firstly, one's mindset plays a pivotal role. Open-mindedness is a critical aspect of embracing TLT's unconventional approach. While it's natural to approach something unfamiliar with a mix of curiosity and caution, being receptive to the process allows for more profound insights and transformations. It's not about blindly accepting every concept but being willing to explore, question, and reflect.

Emotional readiness is another vital component. Engaging with TLT often involves revisiting memories that might have been suppressed or forgotten. Confronting these memories and the associated emotions can be intense. Therefore, ensuring you're in a space where you can safely navigate these emotions is crucial. Suppose you're currently going through significant life stressors or feel emotionally fragile. Discussing your readiness with a therapist or counselor might be beneficial before proceeding with TLT.

The environment during the therapy session plays a substantial role in the overall experience. While the therapist will likely have the right setting for the session, ensuring you feel comfortable and secure is crucial. If the session is conducted remotely, find a quiet, private space where you won't be interrupted. A comforting item, like a blanket or cushion, can also help create a sense of safety.

Lastly, and perhaps most importantly, is the selection of a TLT practitioner. Given the depth and intimacy of the process, it's essential to work with someone certified, experienced, and with whom you feel a genuine connection. Research potential therapists, ask about their qualifications and experience, and consider having an initial consultation to gauge your comfort and alignment with their approach.

In conclusion, Timeline Therapy can offer profound insights, healing, and transformation. However, its effectiveness is significantly influenced by one's preparedness and the practitioner's expertise. By approaching it with an open mind and emotional readiness and ensuring you're in the environment with a skilled therapist, you're setting the stage for a potentially life-changing journey.

Reflection

As part of our human journey, memories from the past, realities from today, and aspirations for tomorrow continually interlace to form our life story. Over time, we realize some chapters bring joyous triumph while others may contain traumas, regrets, or missed opportunities. In understanding and confronting these different threads of our existence, Timeline Therapy (TLT) offers a profound, transformative experience.

Through TLT, we are granted the unique ability to journey across our personal timelines—revisiting moments of hurt, reshaping their impact, and harnessing their lessons. But more than just a voyage going back in time, TLT provides the tools to live with deeper mindfulness in the present, fully engaged and connected with the current moment. By reconciling our past, we free ourselves to truly be present, savoring the richness of life as it unfolds before us.

TLT empowers us to look ahead with clarity and purpose as we stand on the verge of tomorrow. No longer constrained by past grievances or limiting beliefs, we are free to create an inspiring future that aligns with our highest ideals—one where our realities will be tangible, and our goals will not be fantasies.

Yet, for all its transformative potential, TLT is not just a therapeutic modality—it's an invitation. An invitation to embark on the most important journey of all—the journey inward. To explore the landscapes of our mind and soul, confronting shadows, illuminating truths, and rediscovering the essence of who we truly are.

7

CULTIVATING WAYS OF BEING

Throughout human history, the search for comfort in the face of pain has been a shared odyssey. For me personally, I took various paths as I desperately searched to fill that deep sense of emptiness. Enmeshment, a tangled web of connections, was yet another escape I sought to fill the void in my heart that only God could truly satisfy.

As the world faced the pandemic's shadow, I struggled to sleep. CBD/THC gummies and alcohol were used regularly. To combat the weariness of nocturnal shifts, Adderall, borrowed from friends, became my companion. I used leftover pain medication; before I knew it, I was on substances nearly around the clock. Numbing helped me not to feel, but I was a walking wreck when I was off the medications. Racing thoughts robbed me of rest, leading me to more desperate measures. Officers arrived at my house for a wellness check after numerous unanswered calls and messages. My body had given up, and I needed to do something different, or else I was convinced I would die early. My body and soul cried out for change.

In 2016, I was diagnosed with Severe Obstructive Sleep Apnea. Single at the time, I feared that no one would want to marry Darth Vader. My wife and I even joked about that while we were dating. I slept in the living room and asked a question that only a woman of discernment could answer. "Do you have any distilled water?" She asked, "for what? Do you use a CPAP?" She later called my now father-in-law (who also used a CPAP) and vowed never to date or marry anyone who snores.

However, my challenges did not end there. Post-traumatic stress cast an ever-looming shadow over my life—activities that once filled me with joy, like basketball, family gatherings, and exploration, became impossible tasks; depression gradually crept in from behind. By 2021, this darkness had almost driven me over the edge; my spiritual sustenance was reduced to occasional fill ups.

As despair gripped me further, new distractions threatened to shatter my sense of identity; my priorities became numbing and escaping from feeling. While I believed I was steering the ship, I drifted closer to an abyss. Yet, a move to Idaho signaled a pivotal shift. In this new land, surrounded by nature, I found the courage to face my inner commotion. In a profound act of surrender, I embarked on a journey to cultivate a way of being that would allow the fractured pieces of my soul to heal under the nurturing embrace of light and love.

States of Being

In the fabric of human life are threads that elevate our experience from simply existing to profound states of being, often marked by elevated consciousness, deeper understanding, and unwavering presence. States of being that help guide us toward lives filled with purpose, contentment, and true connection. Yet, for many, this state remains difficult to achieve, only catching a glimpse of the possibility.

These pages represent an exploration of these profound states of being. Together, we'll discover what it means to not just exist but to truly be—to be present, connected, and in a state of flow and understanding with the universe around and within us. However, as with any worthwhile pursuit, this state does not appear by accident; instead, it requires intention, dedication, and practice for this journey to bear fruit.

Cultivating these qualities is more than a personal quest for inner calm; it's an influential, transformative force that ripples outward into our interactions, relationships, and, ultimately, the world. By nurturing ourselves internally, we become beacons of peace, understanding, and love that impact our immediate surroundings and humanity.

With today's hectic pace and abundance of distractions, now is the time to embrace these elevated states of being. Now is our opportunity to grow, mature, and realize our fullest potential as individuals and global stewards. Let us embark on this journey together to discover both depths of existence and heights of possibility!

Love: The Universal Binder

At its core, love binds us together. It's the force that acts as the foundation of our most cherished relationships and memories. It is the language that transcends cultures, religions, and lifetimes, holding a unique place in the collection of human emotions. From the love shared between parents and their children to the bonds of friendships and the passions of romantic relationships, love's forms are varied, but its essence remains the same: a profound connection.

Yet, in our day-to-day lives, love can sometimes seem complicated. We face barriers—some external and some of our own making—that can obstruct our understanding of this essential emotion. Past wounds, societal pressures, or personal insecurities might hinder our ability to fully give or receive love. For instance, a past betrayal might make us cautious of opening our hearts again, or societal norms might dictate who we should love and how. Recognizing these barriers is important because understanding them is the first step in navigating around or breaking them down.

However, one of the most transformative understandings of love begins with the self. How we view ourselves and treat ourselves sets the stage for our interactions with others. If we are harsh or judgmental towards ourselves, it becomes difficult to approach others with genuine love and understanding. Activities like reflective journaling, meditation, or daily affirmations can benefit. They can serve as reminders and tools to nurture a sense of self-love.

Cultivating self-love is a foundation enabling us to express love more freely and genuinely to others. It's about grand gestures and everyday acts—listening intently, showing empathy, or extending kindness. It's seeing the good in others, even when hidden, and celebrating the shared human experience.

In essence, love, the universal binder, has the power to connect us, heal us, and elevate our human experience. While the paths to expressing and experiencing love might differ for each of us, its importance remains constant. Through understanding, introspection, and conscious practice, we can harness the boundless potential of love, enriching our lives and the world around us.

Peace

Imagine a tranquil harbor where the waters are calm despite the stormy seas surrounding it. This is the essence of peace—an inner sanctuary that remains undisturbed, no matter the external chaos.

First and foremost, it's essential to differentiate between external and internal peace. External peace refers to the absence of conflict and disruption in our surroundings. It's the peace treaties between nations, the serene environments we sometimes find ourselves in, and the harmonious relationships we foster. While this peace is crucial, it's not always within our control.

On the other hand, internal peace is about cultivating a state of calm and equilibrium within ourselves. It's the ability to remain centered in the face of adversity and not be swayed by fleeting emotions or external pressures. It's about finding that harbor within us. This form of peace is within our control and, arguably, is the more profound of the two. Even in the middle of external chaos, with true inner peace, one can find clarity, resilience, and a sense of purpose.

How, then, can we nurture this inner calm?

1. **Prayer & Meditation:** One of the most recommended practices, mindfulness, is about staying present. It's about observing our thoughts and feelings without judgment. As we practice, we become more attuned to our inner selves, recognizing disruptive patterns and gently guiding our minds back to calm.

2. **Deep Breathing Exercises:** The simple act of breathing deeply can be incredibly grounding. In moments of stress or overwhelm, taking a few deep breaths can reset our nervous system and provide a moment of clarity.

3. **Limiting Stimuli:** We're constantly bombarded with information in our digital age. Taking breaks from screens, practicing digital detoxes, or simply finding

moments of silence can significantly benefit our mental well-being.

4. **Nature Walks:** There's a soothing quality to nature. The rustle of leaves, birds chirping, or a stream's gentle flow can be meditative. Spending time in nature, even if it's just a short walk, can be rejuvenating.

Peace offers us a refuge from the storms of life. While external peace might not always be in our hands, internal peace is a state we can cultivate with intention and practice.

Joy: The Heart's Song

Joy, in its most genuine form, is like a spontaneous song of the heart. That deep feeling springs forth without any particular reason, filling our entire being with wonder and delight. Unlike the fleeting moments of pleasure or the conditional states of happiness, joy has a profoundness; it's both grounding and elevating.

While happiness is often linked to specific circumstances, events, or objects, joy differs. Imagine happiness as the reaction to getting a gift you've wanted. There's delight, of course, and gratitude. But joy? Joy is like the unexpected laughter that bubbles up during an ordinary conversation, the sudden warmth you feel when recalling a fond memory, or the serene contentment of simply being. It's not based on external factors but on our innermost self.

That's not to say that happiness is trivial. On the contrary, happiness is essential and adds color to our lives. But while happiness is reactive, joy is innate. It's a part of our essence, waiting to be tapped into and expressed. And the beauty of joy is that it's accessible to everyone, regardless of their external circumstances. So, how can one tap into this innate reservoir of joy?

One of the key gateways is when we're truly present, not lost in past regrets or future anxieties, we're more open to experiencing the fullness of each moment. Even simple acts, like feeling the texture of a petal, savoring a delicious meal, or listening to a melody, can become profound experiences of joy when approached with mindfulness.

Another method is to cultivate gratitude. It's easy to take our daily blessings for granted and focus on what we lack. But when we start counting our blessings, no matter how small, we shift our focus from scarcity to abundance. This shift in perspective can be a powerful encourager for joy.

Additionally, connecting deeply with others—through heartfelt conversations, acts of kindness, or shared experiences—can be a source of immense joy. Humans are social beings, and meaningful connections can nurture our souls in ways material possessions can't.

Joy is our heart's natural song, a melody that plays effortlessly when we're in tune with our authentic selves. It's not about seeking external validation or chasing temporary pleasures but about aligning with our inner truth and embracing each moment with openness and wonder.

Patience: The Silent Strength

Patience is an icon of silent strength in today's fast-paced society with its attraction to instant gratification. We're so often conditioned to seek out quick fixes and immediate results that the act of waiting, of showing restraint, almost seems outdated. Yet, as anyone who has ever watched a sunrise or patiently nurtured a plant will tell you, some of the most beautiful moments in life unfold in their own time.

Impatience is a symptom of our times. We tap our fingers when the internet lags for a few seconds, honk horns in traffic after a momentary pause, and grow restless waiting for a text reply delayed by just a few minutes. These triggers, small as they might seem, reveal an underlying discomfort with stillness, with the very act of waiting.

Recognizing our triggers of impatience is the first step towards managing them. Often, it's not the act of waiting that's bothersome but the narrative we attach to it. For instance, if we're stuck in traffic, it's not the delay but the story we tell ourselves about the delay—"I'm always unlucky," "This is a waste of my time," "I should've left earlier"—that causes distress. By becoming aware of these narratives, we can challenge and change them and eliminate impatience altogether.

But how does one truly cultivate patience? Like any other virtue, it requires practice. It's about consciously choosing to respond rather than react, to pause and not rush. Simple exercises can help us enhance our resilience and composure. For instance, the next time you're in line, try taking deep breaths and grounding yourself in the present instead of reaching for your phone or getting lost in a spiral of impatient thoughts. Or, when faced with a delay, use that time for reflection, mindfulness, and simply being.

Another powerful tool is empathy. Understanding the bigger picture or placing ourselves in another's shoes can foster patience. If someone is late to meet you, instead of fuming with impatience, consider potential reasons for their delay, thereby cultivating understanding.

Patience is not just about waiting; it's about how we wait. It's an opportunity to demonstrate grace, practice resilience, and fully embrace each moment. Patience is the thread that weaves through our experiences, enriching them with depth and meaning. It's a silent strength that endows us with the capacity to face life's challenges with dignity and composure.

The Interconnection

When our emotions and virtues are in harmony, it can lead to a life of profound fulfillment. Love, peace, joy, and patience are not standalone entities isolated from one another. Instead, they are connected, each amplifying and sustaining each other.

Imagine a world filled with love but no patience. Love might be quick to ignite but equally swift to burn out in the face of challenges. On the other hand, patience nourishes love, allowing it to grow deeper roots, withstand the storms, and blossom in its own time. In this nurturing environment, love thrives and becomes more resilient.

Now, let's consider peace. In many ways, peace is the foundation upon which love and joy are built. It is the calm harbor that provides refuge from life's turbulent waves. When we are at peace within, we create space in our hearts to truly love, to feel joy more intensely, and to demonstrate patience even when tested. Without peace, things would crumble away quickly enough, not allowing love or patience to be shown when needed.

Joy is the spark that ignites when we experience love or find peace in a moment. Yet, patience allows joy to become a sustained melody rather than just a fleeting note. We can savor moments of joy with patience, prolonging them and letting their positive effects ripple into other areas of our lives.

But how does one begin to tap into this interplay? Recognizing the compound benefits of these qualities is a great place to start. When we consciously cultivate one, we inadvertently set the stage for the others to flourish. For instance, by practicing patience in our daily lives, we might find our relationships deepening in love, our minds finding peace more readily, and moments of joy occurring more frequently.

Love, peace, joy, and patience are not just qualities we should aspire to individually. They form an interconnected web, a holistic system that, when balanced, leads to harmonious well-being. By understanding their interplay and consciously nurturing each one, we don't just enhance one aspect of our lives; we elevate our entire human experience.

Change from Within

It's often said that change begins from within, but what is less frequently acknowledged is how deeply our inner transformations can ripple outward, touching everything and everyone in our path. When radiating vibrantly, our internal states can powerfully influence our external realities, creating a chain reaction of positivity and transformation.

Imagine a pond. When a stone is cast into its calm waters, the impact creates ripples that spread far and wide. Similarly, when we embody states like love, peace, joy, and patience, the impact is felt not just within us but also in our interactions, relationships, and even the broader community. We are transmitting waves of positive energy that influence the environment around us.

Our internal states can, and often do, mold the world around us. When we operate from genuine love, we foster deeper connections and understanding. Peaceful interactions lead to reduced conflicts, not just in our immediate surroundings but also in the broader community. Radiating joy has the potential to uplift those around us, creating pockets of happiness in an often chaotic world. Patience, too, has its share, fostering understanding and tolerance in diverse settings.

Techniques to Embody and Radiate These Qualities

Maintaining a state of balanced well-being can often feel like a challenge. However, through a combination of intentional practices, we can embody love, peace, joy, and patience and radiate these qualities, influencing our surroundings. Here are some techniques to help us anchor and amplify these profound states of being.

Mindfulness and Meditation:

Rooted in ancient traditions and validated by modern science, mindfulness and meditation serve as potent tools to cultivate these qualities. For love, one might practice a loving-kindness (Metta) meditation, sending well-wishes first to oneself and then expanding this compassion outward. To foster peace, grounding meditations, which focus on the present moment and bodily sensations, can be incredibly effective. For joy, meditative practices that hone in on gratitude can elicit feelings of happiness and contentment. And for patience, mindfulness exercises that challenge us to observe without judgment—whether it's our breath, thoughts, or external stimuli—can strengthen our patience muscles.

Visualizations and Affirmations:

The mind is a powerful entity. By visualizing scenarios where we embody these qualities, we prepare ourselves to act in alignment with them. Imagine a day filled with joyous moments, or envision yourself calmly navigating a challenging situation. Accompany these visualizations with affirmations: positive, present-tense statements like "I am filled with love" or "I exude peace in every situation." Repeated regularly, these affirmations can rewire our neural pathways, making accessing and radiating these qualities easier.

Daily Rituals:

Simple, daily rituals can serve as reminders and reinforcers. It might be as straightforward as starting each day with a moment of gratitude, thus setting a joyous tone, or it could be a nightly reflection on acts of patience exhibited throughout the day. These rituals, while small, compound over time and gradually become ingrained in our minds.

Creative Outlets:

Art, in all its forms, provides a medium to express and further cultivate these qualities. Drawing, painting, or doodling can be meditative, allowing us to tap into peace. Writing love letters, even if just to oneself, can deepen our sense of love and connection.

Music, whether listening to or creating it, can elicit a wide range of emotions, from joy to tranquility. Engaging in these creative ways provides an outlet and amplifies our connection to love, peace, joy, and patience.

Incorporating these techniques into our lives doesn't demand drastic changes. Instead, it's about making small, intentional shifts in our daily routines and mindsets. Over time, these shifts accumulate, allowing us to embody these states of being and shine brightly, radiating love, peace, joy, and patience into the world.

Challenges and Triumphs on the Journey

Starting a journey to cultivate deeper states of love, peace, joy, and patience is rewarding and challenging. Like any meaningful endeavor, this path is not always linear. Instead, it resembles the flow of an ocean's tide: moments of profound connection scattered with phases where these desired states may seem unattainable.

Every individual, regardless of their dedication to personal growth, will encounter challenges. Life is unpredictable, throwing curveballs that may momentarily shake one's commitment to these states of being. External pressures, past traumas, or daily stresses can sometimes cloud our ability to consistently embody love or maintain inner peace. These fluctuations are natural, and acknowledging them is the first step towards gracefully navigating them.

However, every challenge also offers a silver lining. Setbacks, when viewed through the lens of growth, transform into opportunities. They become powerful teachers, guiding us to better understand ourselves and our emotions. For instance, a momentary lapse in patience can serve as a reminder of areas still needing attention. By embracing and learning from these challenges, we grow stronger and develop a profound sense of resilience.

During these challenges, it's important to celebrate the small victories. Every moment of genuine joy, every day where peace prevails, and every instance where love and patience guide our actions should be acknowledged and cherished. No matter how seemingly insignificant, these triumphs fuel our journey forward, reminding us of our capacity for profound inner transformation.

In pursuit of these elevated states of being, it's crucial to arm oneself with determination and compassion. When the journey feels challenging, leaning on supportive communities, practices, or guidance can be invaluable. Remember, striving for these states is not about perfection but progress. It's a journey of challenges and triumphs, with each step, setback, or success bringing us closer to our most authentic selves.

Reflection

By prioritizing and practicing these states of being, we unlock the potential for a seismic shift in our perspectives. The challenges we once viewed as impossible can transform into avenues of growth; moments of despair can be overshadowed by instances of incomparable joy. We are cultivating an internal sanctuary, a resilient core that remains unshaken despite external chaos. But the impact of this journey doesn't stop at personal transformation. As we embody these qualities, our actions, decisions, and interactions radiate with the same energy, touching the lives of those around us. Our positivity influences our families, communities, and even strangers with the warmth of our presence.

This transformative potential is not exclusive; it's calling to each of us, urging us to tap into the reservoirs of love, peace, joy, and patience that lie dormant within. Commit to this transformative journey not just for personal growth but as a testament to the beauty and harmony you can bring into the world. Because in nurturing these states within, we hold the power to craft a world rich in compassion, understanding, and shared joy.

8

CREATING AN ENVIRONMENT FOR TRANSFORMATION

At the height of the COVID crisis, as fear and uncertainty gripped the world, I walked a delicate path of responsibility and commitment, not just as a healthcare worker but as a family man. With the introduction of COVID-19 tests, a shimmer of hope for safety dawned. Yet, for those in the healthcare industry like me, this sense of security was dimmed by layers of bureaucracy. As someone dedicated to the safety of patients, colleagues, and most importantly, my family, I felt a sense of duty to get tested when I exhibited alarming symptoms like chest tightness and shortness of breath.

Seeking approval from our assistant manager for testing was not just about my well-being; it was a proactive step in ensuring I wouldn't unintentionally harm others. Yet, in this tight-knit world of our respiratory department, my genuine concerns were misinterpreted. Whispers filled the hallways, suggesting I was seeking an escape from the frontline or betraying my colleagues in the thick of this war against an unseen enemy.

Behind the scenes, there was another narrative that many were perhaps unaware of. My wife was on the cusp of bringing our second child into this world, and our 14-month-old daughter was still navigating her first steps. At that moment, my roles as a dedicated healthcare worker and a protective father and husband merged.

Though relief washed over me when my test results were negative, the atmosphere at work had palpably shifted during my 10-day isolation. Whispers had grown louder, casting doubts on my integrity and questioning my dedication. The camaraderie and support that once characterized my workplace had now been replaced by skepticism and distrust.

This phase, presented with emotional and relational challenges, became transformative in my life. It underscored the significance of standing tall in the face of adversity, cultivating an environment of understanding and trust, even when surrounded by doubt. This ordeal taught me the profound lesson of moving forward with resilience and grace, even when the path is uncertain.

Our internal world often reflects and is reflected by our external environment. It's an intrinsic rhythm that we're usually unaware of its profound impact. As we journey through different phases of life, our surroundings play a pivotal role, acting either as a catalyst or an impediment to our personal growth and transformation.

Consider for a moment the role of a gardener, precisely crafting an environment good for a plant's growth. The soil's nutrient content, the amount of sunlight, and the pot's size can determine how well a plant thrives. Similarly, our surroundings—the people we surround ourselves with, the spaces we inhabit, or the routines we adopt—can nourish or hinder our aspirations. It's a dynamic balance in which our surroundings can echo our internal struggles and joys, just as our inner state can shape how we perceive and interact with the world outside.

As we explore further in this chapter, we'll understand how, by being mindful of our environment and making intentional changes, we can foster conditions that not only support our personal evolution but also amplify it.

Environmental Psychology

At the intersection of our external surroundings and our inner psyche lies a dynamic field known as environmental psychology. This exciting field examines how physical environments influence human cognition, emotions, and behaviors. Through exploring this relationship more fully, it becomes evident that our surroundings don't simply serve as backdrops but actively influence both mindsets and well-being.

Scientific studies have consistently shown the profound impact that environments can have on our mental processes. For instance, natural light in a workspace can significantly boost productivity, enhance mood, and reduce fatigue. Similarly, urban residents with access to green spaces report lower levels of stress, improved mood, and better overall mental health. All of this evidence reveals the fact that our surroundings play a direct role in influencing our brain's function and emotional state.

Environmental psychology explores these correlations further, investigating why certain settings might induce feelings of tranquility while others can cause tension. The design of a space, its colors, its acoustic properties, and even its scent can influence our emotions and behaviors in subtle yet significant ways. For instance, the color blue is often associated with calmness and can reduce heart rates. While red hues can evoke excitement or even agitation.

But it's not just about the physical attributes. Our connection to spaces, infused with memories or societal associations, further shapes our reactions. A place that reminds us of a cherished childhood memory might produce warmth and nostalgia. At the same time, a setting that looks similar to where a traumatic event occurred might stir feelings of discomfort or anxiety.

By understanding the science behind the environment and mindset, we can more strategically create spaces that not only support our aspirations but also actively facilitate our growth. Whether it's a quiet corner for introspection, a vibrant room for creativity, or a serene space for relaxation, the environments we create and inhabit can be powerful allies in our quest for holistic evolution.

Our surroundings can act as a mirror, reflecting our internal states. When we encounter a cluttered room, it can bring forth feelings of chaos, and a poorly lit environment might dampen our spirits. On the other hand, spaces designed thoughtfully can elevate our moods, inspire creativity, and foster a sense of tranquility. When we curate spaces that sing, we're not just organizing our physical realm, but we're also setting the stage for our personal growth and transformation.

A Personal Touch to Your Space

Key elements in a space that can make it feel like serenity include natural light, soothing colors, and comfortable furniture. Imagine the warmth of sunlight streaming through a window, filling a room painted in soft pastels adorned with cushions and throws. Such an environment immediately envelops you in a cocoon of comfort and peace, facilitating reflection and relaxation.

However, it's not just about aesthetics but functionality, too. Decluttering, a concept popularized by Marie Kondo, is more than an organizational exercise. It's a symbolic act of letting go of the old to make way for the new. By decluttering, we remove the physical (and often emotional) baggage that holds us back, creating spaces that breathe. Practical steps include categorizing items, discarding or donating what no longer serves us, and organizing the rest in a way that's both functional and pleasing to the eye.

Infusing personal touches into your space is important. Incorporating elements of nature, be it through house plants, a bubbling fountain, or even sounds of nature playing in the background, can reconnect us to the earth and its grounding energies. Art, too, plays a role. Whether a painting that speaks to you, a sculpture that intrigues you, or even photographs of cherished memories, art can create emotions, inspire thoughts, and stimulate creativity.

Lastly, personal memorabilia, like heirlooms, souvenirs from travels, or even books, can make a space your own. These items tell your story and anchor you to your journey, reminding you of where you've been and where you aspire to go.

Designing spaces encouraging growth is like creating a sanctuary. In this haven, your soul feels nurtured, your mind is invigorated, and your spirit is free to soar. By paying attention to the details and making conscious choices, we can transform any area into a trigger for personal evolution.

Awakening Our Senses

Our sensory experiences play a role in shaping our emotions, perceptions, and overall well-being. A familiar scent can transport us back in time, a specific song can uplift our spirits, and the softness of a blanket can wrap us in comfort. The ambient stimuli surrounding us are not just passive elements; they actively shape our internal world.

Sounds, particularly music, can have an almost magical impact on our minds. Consider how intense emotions may arise while listening to an emotional symphony or the peace experienced during a meditative chant. Music has the power to resonate with our souls, making it a valuable tool for personal growth. By creating playlists that mirror our aspirations, we can create an auditory environment open to reflection, motivation, and healing.

Whether it's the tranquil notes of nature sounds for meditation or the energizing beats of a workout playlist, music can be harnessed to support our goals.

Scent has a profound impact on our state of being. Aromatherapy, the therapeutic use of plant-derived, aromatic essential oils, has been recognized for its potential to balance, harmonize, and promote the health of body, mind, and spirit. For instance, lavender is known for its calming properties, while citrus scents like lemon or orange can invigorate and uplift. By selecting fragrances that align with our current needs—relaxation, focus, or energy—we can craft an olfactory landscape that nurtures our journey.

Tactile experiences also significantly influence our mood and mindset. The textures we surround ourselves with, be it the softness of a cushion, the graininess of a wooden table, or the smoothness of silk, engage our sense of touch, drawing out a range of emotions. Creating a tactile environment that supports personal transformation might involve selecting materials that provide comfort, warmth, and safety. A plush rug underfoot, a cozy throw on a sofa, or even the weight of a comforting weighted blanket can add sensory support to our spaces.

The ambiance we create through sounds, scents, and sensations is a powerful backdrop for our transformation journey. Mindfully selecting and integrating these sensory experiences into our environment, we set the stage for a deeper connection with ourselves, facilitating growth, introspection, and well-being.

Technology

In today's modern world, our online presence and the digital spaces we frequent have become an extension of our day-to-day lives. The screens we gaze upon, the notifications we receive, and the virtual communities we engage in can enrich our lives or take away from our well-being. Understanding the deep influence of these digital realms is crucial for those on a path of personal transformation.

Digital environments, especially social media platforms, have a dual nature. On one hand, they can provide inspiration, connection, and knowledge. Platforms can introduce us to different cultures and innovative ideas or unite us with like-minded individuals. On the other hand, they can also be a source of comparison, misinformation, and negativity. The constant intake of highlights from others' lives, the controversial debates, or simply the overwhelming volume of content can be mentally and emotionally draining.

It's essential to engage in regular digital detoxes when navigating the digital world efficiently. This means periodically reviewing and decluttering our online subscriptions, friend lists, and the apps we use. By being intentional with whom and what we engage with, we can ensure that our digital interactions align more with our transformation goals. For instance, following accounts or joining groups that inspire personal growth, positivity, and genuine connection can create a nourishing online atmosphere.

However, as enriching as the digital world can be, it's equally important to ground ourselves in the tangible, physical world. While online interactions offer a sense of community, they can never fully replace the depth and warmth of face-to-face human connections. Taking deliberate breaks from screens—walking in nature, engaging in a hobby, or simply practicing mindfulness—can help rejuvenate the mind and provide a refreshing contrast to the pixelated world.

Moreover, the blue light released from screens, especially late at night, can disrupt our natural sleep patterns. Designating tech-free zones in our homes or setting aside specific times during the day when devices are off-limits can help reduce this effect and create a more balanced relationship with our devices.

In sum, while the digital age presents many opportunities and resources for growth, it's important to approach it with discernment. By thoughtfully choosing our online environments and ensuring they serve our highest good while valuing and prioritizing real-world experiences, we can strike a harmonious balance, achieving genuine transformation.

Choosing Your People

Human beings are intrinsically social creatures. We thrive on interaction, validation, and shared experiences. Historically, it was within the community that individuals found protection, learned social norms, and cultivated a sense of belonging. In the context of personal transformation, surrounding oneself with a community that champions growth-centric values becomes necessary. Such communities can be a source of encouragement during challenging times, offer diverse perspectives, and serve as a reservoir of collective wisdom.

To foster enriching connections, one might consider joining clubs, workshops, or groups aligned with their interests and aspirations. This could range from book clubs, yoga classes, and group meditations to workshops on self-development, leadership, or any area that feeds one's passion. In these settings, it's likely to find kindred spirits—individuals who, too, are on their own transformative journeys and value the mutual exchange of support and inspiration.

However, when seeking out positive relationships, it's equally crucial to recognize and distance ourselves from bonds that are toxic or detrimental to our growth. These relationships are often characterized by consistent negativity, lack of support, or even subtle forms of manipulation. The energy drain they cause can be a significant roadblock to personal evolution. Here, setting boundaries becomes key. This doesn't necessarily mean cutting ties immediately or entirely but could involve taking a step back, limiting interaction, or openly communicating one's feelings and needs.

Remember that as we grow and evolve, our social circles might change, and that's natural. Some relationships may deepen, while others may fade. This is all part of the transformation process. By consciously choosing communities that resonate with our higher selves and align with our growth goals, we set the stage for deeper connections and more profound insights. Embracing relationships that nurture the spirit and learning to let go of those that don't is a testament to one's commitment to personal evolution.

Boundaries

In our journey toward transformation and personal growth, we must recognize that not every external influence serves our best interest. Just as a gardener sets up fences to protect delicate plants from pests, we, too, must establish boundaries to protect and nurture ourselves. These boundaries, both tangible and intangible, act as safeguards, ensuring that our transformative space remains receptive to growth and well-being.

Setting boundaries is not about shutting out the world but determining which influences we allow to enter our lives. They are deeply personal, varying from individual to individual, based on past experiences, current needs, and future aspirations. For some, it might mean designating uninterrupted time for self-reflection or meditation. For others, it might involve distancing from individuals or situations that drain emotional energy.

To effectively set boundaries, clear and assertive communication is important. It's about articulating needs without being aggressive or passive. For instance, if someone consistently interrupts your early morning quiet time, you might say, "I value our conversations, but I've set aside mornings for personal reflection. Is it cool if we chat in the afternoon instead?" By doing so, you're not only communicating your boundary but also expressing the importance of that protected time to your well-being.

However, setting boundaries is just the first step. Their real strength lies in upholding them consistently. It's natural for boundaries to be tested, knowingly or unknowingly, by external forces. In such instances, recognizing signs of boundary violations is crucial. This could manifest as feelings of discomfort, resentment, or even burnout. When you sense these emotions, it's a signal that your boundaries might be getting compromised.

Remember to take corrective measures when boundaries are broken. This doesn't always mean confrontation. Often, a simple reminder can do the trick. In other situations, you might need to distance yourself temporarily or permanently from the source of the violation.

Boundaries are neither rigid walls nor barriers. They are fluid, evolving with our changing needs and circumstances. It is beneficial to understand why they exist: to protect our transformative journey. By setting and honoring these boundaries, we ensure our personal growth space remains untainted. And in doing so, we not only protect our own well-being but also model the importance of self-care and respect for others.

Empathy and Active Listening

Empathy and active listening stand as cornerstones of transformative environments. These qualities not only enable individuals to deeply connect with others but also foster spaces of understanding, trust, and mutual growth. These skills allow us to step into another's shoes, perceive their emotions, and respond in a manner that validates and supports them.

Empathy is more than just feeling for someone; it's about feeling with them. When we genuinely empathize, we mirror another's emotions, allowing ourselves to momentarily experience their joy, pain, or confusion. This shared emotional state, even if it's brief, bridges gaps of misunderstanding and strengthens interpersonal connections. For instance, if your friend shares their anxieties about an event coming up soon—an effective, empathetic response might include both understanding their nervousness as well as feeling their stress before providing appropriate relief measures that soothe their concerns.

Active listening complements empathy by ensuring that we genuinely hear and understand the spoken words, underlying emotions, and unvoiced sentiments. It involves fully concentrating, understanding, and responding to the person speaking rather than just passively 'hearing' the message. By practicing active listening, we signal to the other person that their feelings and perspectives are valid and valuable.

For example, one might share concerns about feeling unfulfilled at work. An active listener wouldn't just nod or provide solutions, but they would dig deeper, asking open-ended questions, summarizing their understanding, and sharing similar experiences, resulting in mutual trust and respect.

To enhance these skills, engaging in a few practical exercises helps. Role-playing scenarios with a friend or colleague can be beneficial. One person can share a story or concern, while the other practices active listening, ensuring they don't interrupt, offering feedback only when asked, and summarizing the main points at the end. Another exercise is the "Empathy Circle," where participants take turns speaking on a topic, and others reflect back on what they've understood, fostering both empathy and active listening.

Incorporating empathy and active listening into daily interactions creates environments where individuals feel seen, heard, and valued. Such spaces become fertile ground for personal transformation. When our feelings and perspectives are respected, we are more open to sharing, learning, and growing. Empathy and active listening is not just about effective communication; it's key in crafting transformative environments.

Reflection

As life unfolds, we experience and encounter diverse experiences, continuous learning, challenges, and triumphs. One constant in life remains: change is unavoidable. With each passing year comes new environments to adapt or reconfigure to match our inner growth; ensuring they reflect this is a constant effort that echoes life's ever-evolving seasons.

Much like nature, our personal landscapes undergo transformations. There are times in spring when everything feels new and full of potential. Then come the summers of abundance, where we relax in the warmth of our achievements. Fall might bring in a period of reflection and gratitude, while winter could be a time of rest, rejuvenation, or facing challenges.

Another crucial aspect is remaining attuned to our inner selves. Often, our emotions, body, and intuition signal when an environment is misaligned with our current growth phase. Feelings of restlessness, stagnation, or discomfort are cues prompting us to re-evaluate and realign.

Moreover, it's beneficial to set aside dedicated time, perhaps at the beginning or end of each year, for a holistic environmental review. This can be a moment to reflect on the past, envision the future, and outline steps to adapt our surroundings accordingly. For instance, if a significant life change is on the horizon, such as pursuing higher education, starting a family, or shifting careers, anticipate the environmental shifts needed to support this new phase.

Embracing the fluidity of life and the necessity for adaptation doesn't signify instability or inconsistency. Instead, it's a testament to our resilience, awareness, and commitment to personal growth. As we journey through life's varied seasons, our environments should be our allies, not adversaries. By continuously adapting them to our evolving selves, we ensure they remain promoters for transformation, helping our journey toward the best versions of ourselves.

Embracing fluidity in our environmental design is like dancing with life. It's about allowing ourselves to flow with change rather than resisting it. It's realizing that, much like a river that constantly changes yet remains true to its nature, we can redesign, recreate, and rearrange our environments without losing our core identity.

We have explored the science, psychology, and art of environments and their profound impact on our transformative processes. We've navigated creating spaces that resonate with growth, serenity, and positivity. We've understood the immense power of sensory experiences, digital realms, and the communities we choose. We must acknowledge that crafting an environment for transformation isn't a one-time act but an ongoing process.

To every reader, look around you and ask, "Does this space reflect who I am? Does it support where I want to go?" Know that every element, every corner, every chosen object or discarded item tells a story. Make it a story of transformation, growth, and conscious evolution. Embrace the dynamic dance of life, adapting and reshaping your environments as you flow through its many experiences.

May we all recognize and harness the transformative potential of our surroundings. Let's craft spaces that nurture our spirits, inspire our minds, and cradle our dreams. Through intention and action, let's make our environments the fertile ground from which our best selves can bloom.

DIVINE WHISPER

If I don't heal it, it'll be on him.

Before every breakthrough, there's a burden ripe and ready to be let go. That's where the sweet fruit shows up. Writing poetry allows me to enjoy the trial:

Another day, another fight
Stay up all day, been up all night,
Back to the drill
Three strikes I'm out,
Another storm
Or self-made drought?
These pitch black days,
Phone screens at night
My lustful flesh,
No candlelight.
Broken from burdens
I think I'm strong!
Instead of sleep,

I hit that bong.

Then hella sips

Feel less and less

Runnin' out of breath

Like full court press.

Lord, come and save me

My soul's a mess

Brain fogged with clouds

Body stuck in stress.

One day at a time,

You can't do that!

Start with an hour,

Man I can't keep track!

"Then take a breath,

It's my gift to you!"

God whispered louder,

"Just let me through!"

God save me now,

Ill do what you say!

Is that your voice?

Lord God, don't play!

These skies is dark,

My hair turning gray.

Looking in the mirror

Piss poor dismay.

"For each command,

Like a call declined,

You choose the ganja,

Double down with wine.

Son hear me out,

I'm a gentleman,

I speak the truth,

Not like your friends.

My wrath will torch,

Your shame will scream,

Don't burn in hell,

I gave you dreams!

Pray for discernment,

Choose wisdom too,

My patience deep,

Like ocean's blue.

Put your flesh to death

Wasn't Paul once Saul?

Sol's vice was women,

Kobe's basketball.

What you see is fleeting

S'all blasphemy!

Heaven, cause you're Saved?

Luke-warm mediocrity.

Claim faith without works

And your passive praise?

This aint Roaring Springs,

talking Heaven's Gates!

You're next in line

On Satan's list,

Repent and run!

Ain't no time for bliss.

My son, come home!

One decision away

Faith over fear

A trail you'll blaze

You'll be restored,

I've set you apart,

Substitute your guilt,

wit' a flesh-made heart.

Listen to My words,

All you gotta do,

Pray Trust & Seek.

I Declare you...NEW!"

Testimony

9

SHARING YOUR STORY

In the initial days of the global pandemic, I cared for patients diagnosed with the virus, and three back-to-back shifts became my routine. In those early days, COVID-19 tests were a luxury not all could access, heightening the need for precaution. With the NICU's delicate babies and the families that loved them in mind, I religiously wore my mask during every shift, a small barrier between me and the unseen enemy.

But one day, this practice was disrupted when the charge nurse unexpectedly asked me to remove the mask. Torn between duty and personal conviction, I hesitated but eventually did as asked. It wasn't long after this incident that a worried father, whose premature baby I had assisted in delivering, approached me. His anxiety was palpable, grounded in the tragic memory of losing his first child to a hospital-borne infection.

Taking a deep breath, I shared my truth with him. The widespread belief that "babies can't contract COVID" felt like a misguided comfort to me. My mask, I explained, was my silent pledge to shield the innocent lives in the NICU, including his own child. Stirred by our conversation and driven by an inner calling, I put my mask back on, defying any directive prioritizing the safety of these fragile souls.

In this commitment, I saw a larger purpose, a mission to be the voice for those too small to speak. As days turned into months, it was eventually accepted that even babies weren't immune to the virus's clutches. My intuitive protective stance was vindicated, but it wasn't about being right. It was a profound reminder of God's guiding hand in my life. Guiding me to stand firm, trust my instincts, and be a beacon of hope and care in a crisis.

This episode in my life wasn't just about wearing a mask; it was about understanding the ripple effects of our actions and the transformative power of conviction and compassion.

The Ripple Effect

There exists a phenomenon as powerful as it is subtle: the "ripple effect." Like a single droplet of water sending waves across an entire pond, our actions, choices, and shared experiences can set off a series of reactions, influencing not just our immediate surroundings but extending far beyond what the eye can see. This is the foundation of how we evolve, where an individual's transformation can spark a shift, igniting change across communities and even generations.

Imagine the profound impact of sharing your journey with its trials, triumphs, and learned wisdom. As we open up, we allow others to do the same, creating a chain of vulnerability, understanding, and growth. But it's not just about storytelling. It's about the earnestness in our voices, the authenticity of our tales, and the passion with which we live our truths. By embracing our narratives and sharing them with the world, we unleash a force that can reshape societal norms, challenge established beliefs, and inspire countless others to embark on their journeys of discovery and transformation.

The stories we tell, the experiences we share, and the lessons we impart are not just for us. They become the collective heritage of humanity, with the potential to guide, uplift, and reshape the trajectory of our shared destiny. These "transformation stories" serve not just as short, meaningless stories but as powerful testaments of human resilience as we adapt, change, and move forward together as one society.

But what binds these stories together is not just the transformation itself but the aftermath—the ripples that come out from each transformative moment. Your story shows that transformation isn't an isolated event; it's an ongoing process, influencing every choice, interaction, and endeavor.

Sharing personal stories, laying bare one's soul for the world to see, takes bravery. It's no wonder, then, that many of us deal with fears and resistance when it comes to recounting our stories of transformation. There's a nagging voice inside that whispers, "What will they think?" or "Is my story even worth sharing?" For some, the fear might manifest as a reluctance to appear vulnerable, believing that vulnerability might be mistaken for weakness.

Others might worry about being judged, misunderstood, or mocked.

As I explore the nature of vulnerability, a profound realization emerges: vulnerability is not a sign of weakness but of immense strength. It requires courage to show one's authentic self. Vulnerability has the power to connect, resonate, and forge bonds that are deeply human and authentic.

There's a myth in society that says we need to "have it all together" before we can inspire or guide others. Until we reach a certain point of perfection or achieve a particular milestone, our stories lack validity or value. This notion couldn't be further from the truth. Every journey, regardless of where one is on their path, holds lessons, insights, and inspirations for others. One doesn't need to wait for a grand finale or a neatly tied-up ending to share their narrative.

In reality, the messiness, the in-betweens, and the ongoing nature of personal growth make stories relatable and impactful. It's in these raw, unfiltered moments that others see themselves, drawing comfort from the fact that they aren't alone in their challenges. By debunking the myth of "having it all together," we celebrate the journey's entirety, the highs, and the lows, and acknowledge that every step, no matter how small or uncertain, is a testament to human resilience and spirit.

In embracing vulnerability in visibility, we pave the way for genuine connections, inspire others with our authenticity, and affirm the value of every individual's story. After all, it's not about reaching the destination but about cherishing and sharing the journey that makes a difference.

Imperfect Narrators

In the history of human storytelling, it's often those who stand atop mountains of achievement who get the loudest applause. We praise the victorious, the accomplished, the 'perfected' tales. However, when it comes to stories of personal transformation, there's an unsung beauty and potency in the stories narrated by the "imperfect narrator"—those still on their journey, navigating the challenges and celebrations that come with growth.

Why might someone hesitate to share if they feel they haven't "arrived" yet? Perhaps it's the societal pressure to present the perfect image of success, or maybe it's the internal feeling of inadequacy. But true transformation is a fluid process. It's ongoing, and it doesn't always have a neatly defined beginning, middle, and end. And that is where the charm lies.

By focusing on progress over perfection, we shift our perspective from the destination to the journey itself. Each step, no matter how uncertain, each setback, no matter how discouraging, becomes a valuable part of the narrative. This emphasis creates a space where every twist and turn, every stumble and soar, holds merit. It's a celebration of the continuous effort to evolve rather than just the moments of evident success.

Interestingly, it's often the unfinished, unpolished stories that resonate the most. Why? Because they are real, raw, and relatable.

When someone shares their ongoing struggles and uncertainties alongside their victories, listeners find comfort in the shared human experience. It becomes less about the awe of a grand accomplishment and more about the camaraderie of shared challenges and aspirations.

An imperfect narrator doesn't just recount experiences; they invite others into their world, offering them a front-row seat to their journey. The shared vulnerability, the acknowledgment of flaws, and the open-ended nature of their story often serve as a beacon of hope for others. It conveys a powerful message: "I'm still on my path, figuring things out, and that's okay. You can be, too."

In embracing our roles as imperfect narrators, we contribute to human experiences that are diverse, genuine, and profoundly impactful. After all, while neatly tied conclusions might offer a momentary sense of satisfaction, it's the ongoing sagas, with all their beautiful imperfections, that truly inspire and connect us.

Belonging

Throughout history, our ancestors huddled around campfires, sharing stories of celestial wonders and the mysteries of the unknown. Today, while the nature of our gatherings has evolved, the purpose remains unchanged. We long for connection, understanding, and friendships. We seek reflections of our experiences in others and, in doing so, find belonging.

Human psychology, while complex and varied, shares common threads that link us all. Whether it's the heart-wrenching pain of loss, the dizzying heights of love, the depths of despair, or the celebration of success, certain themes and emotions echo universally. They cross geographical boundaries, cultural divides, and temporal eras, resonating deeply with diverse audiences. This is not coincidental; it's rooted in our shared evolutionary journey, our mutual desires, and our collective struggles.

When someone musters the courage to share a personal story of transformation, it often strikes a chord with listeners not because of the specifics but because of these underlying universal emotions. A person in a city might find friendship with someone from a remote village, not because they've walked in each other's shoes but because they've felt similar emotions—perhaps longing, joy, disappointment, or hope.

An awareness that one isn't alone can provide great comfort in times of challenge; understanding can provide healing for wounded souls or light in moments of darkness, reminding us all that while our paths might differ, emotions shared along the way do not. Your narrative could become part of a web of collective experiences fostering empathy and deepening connections with people you don't even know personally.

Sharing Your Message

In today's highly connected world, various methods are available for individuals to share their stories of transformation, ranging from personal one-on-one conversations to global platforms accessible to millions. The choice of platform can profoundly influence not only the reach of the story but also the depth of its impact.

One of the most intimate ways to share one's journey is through personal conversations. These can occur within the comforting embrace of a close-knit circle, be it with family, friends, or small support groups. There's immediate feedback in the form of nods, tears, smiles, or comforting touches. However, the depth and richness of these face-to-face exchanges might come at the cost of limited reach.

On the other hand, the digital age has revolutionized our ability to share and connect. Blogging, for instance, allows individuals to pen down their transformative journeys, allowing for reflection, elaboration, and a touch of creativity. Written words have the ability to produce powerful feelings, insights, and epiphanies that can reach readers across the globe. Similarly, podcasts have emerged as a dynamic medium where voices narrate stories of change, challenges, and triumphs, bringing a sense of intimacy to listeners.

Social media platforms, with numerous user bases, offer a worldwide reach. From bite-sized transformational narratives on Twitter to visual stories on Instagram, there's a space for every kind of storyteller. However, the immensity of these platforms can also pose challenges. The narrative might get lost in the noise, or the feedback might not always be constructive.

Choosing the right platform requires introspection. One must ask themselves: What's my primary goal? Is it a deep connection, widespread reach, or a blend of both? It's crucial to select a platform that aligns with one's comfort level, storytelling style, and desired audience engagement.

Once the platform is chosen, effectively communicating becomes important. For personal conversations, active listening and empathy is key. For written platforms, honing one's writing skills, being authentic, and engaging with readers can amplify the impact. In podcasts, speech clarity, pacing, and a touch of emotion can captivate listeners.

The art of sharing one's transformative journey is not just about the story itself but also how and where it's told. By thoughtfully choosing and leveraging platforms, storytellers can ensure their stories of transformation ripple out, touching, inspiring, and connecting with countless souls across the globe.

Reflection

Sharing personal journeys and experiences is, at its core, a profound exchange of energy between the storyteller and the listener or reader. Sharing is not a one-dimensional act. When we open up about our transformative experiences, we express and release pent-up emotions, bringing a sense of catharsis. This expression, like an artist painting on a canvas, is a deep joy in itself. It allows for introspection, validation, and sometimes, even closure. By vocalizing or documenting our journey, we often view it through a fresh lens, seeing patterns, insights, and lessons that might have previously not been seen before.

On the other side of this exchange is the listener or reader. They, too, are on a journey, perhaps seeking inspiration and guidance. The ripple effect of one story can impact countless lives, making them reflect and change. However, with the joys of sharing come its challenges. Not all feedback is positive. Some might misunderstand, misinterpret, or even criticize our experiences and choices. In such moments, it's essential to stay anchored in one's truth. Every transformative journey is deeply personal, and while feedback is valuable, it's crucial to sift through it, retaining what resonates and letting go of what doesn't.

Every story carries within it the seeds of change. Even the simplest recounting of a personal challenge and the following triumph can resonate deeply with a listener or reader. It might inspire them to face their fears, change an ingrained habit, or pursue a long-lost dream. Our stories, when shared, become beacons of hope and examples of human resilience and adaptability. They remind others that change, however intimidating, is possible and within reach.

Yet, with this recognition comes a profound sense of responsibility. When we realize that our stories can produce change, we are entrusted with sharing them authentically and responsibly. This means being truthful, reflective, and mindful of the impact our words can have. It also means understanding that while our story can spark change, everyone's transformative journey will be uniquely shaped by their experiences, beliefs, and circumstances.

In encouraging others to embark on their transformative journeys, it's essential to offer support without imposition of guidance or directives. Our role is not to dictate the path for others but to illuminate potential routes they can explore. It's about offering a hand, a word of encouragement, or a listening ear when needed. By doing so, we allow others to discover and define their own paths.

Please take a moment to honor your journey in all its complexity. Understand that your story, regardless of its scale or scope, has the power to impact. Whether it's a whispered secret to a confidant, a penned journal entry, or a story recounted to a gathering, let your voice be heard. Sharing could spark change for someone else!

10

———

Authenticity, Vulnerability, and Resonance

I n the quest for authenticity, standing against the tide or
questioning established norms demands courage. It's like
stepping onto a battlefield, armed only with convictions and
shielded by unwavering faith. While it's instinctual to seek
refuge and clarity from established hierarchies like senior leaders,
managers, or even therapeutic methods, sometimes, these very
channels can echo back the hollow sound of silence. This was
the maze of emotions and experiences I found myself navigating,
trusting only my intuition among the noise of unanswered
questions.

The paths I took seeking guidance and understanding led
to dead ends. My concerns, genuine and pressing, met with a
heavy silence, making me question my own perceptions. My
world shifted into an unexpected pause—I was placed on an
administrative leave that felt like confinement, especially following
the stay-at-home protocols. With masks delivered to my door and

a cautionary warning to avoid family contact, my isolation became palpable. Like countless others, I was reduced to an observer, watching the world through the lens of the media.

My readiness to rejoin work was met with unforeseen hurdles. My shifts, it turned out, had been reallocated while COVID-19 testing proved inaccessible; as colleagues returned, I deteriorated alone at home during confusing protocols, inexplicable practices, and obvious discord within our respiratory department, the situation appeared impossible to comprehend logically.

Challenging times often rallied teams together, yet our unit was falling apart, each of us confined to our solitary spheres tasked with caring for critically ill patients. Desperate for answers and clarity, I turned to loved ones, acquaintances, and strangers, only to confront a void of understanding. It was here, in the depth of isolation, that I felt an enveloping numbness. Distractions became a salve for my restless mind. The working environment grew toxic, with absent leadership and unclear directives. Deviating from the dictated path risked disciplinary actions, jeopardizing not just our roles but the very sustenance of our families.

Authenticity, vulnerability, and resonance are more than just words. These words give life to our stories and journeys. They also give voice to the silent battles we fight. Authenticity is the art of being unapologetically ourselves, of showing up in our truth even when it's uncomfortable or goes against the grain. Vulnerability is the courage to bare our souls, to let our guard down, and to admit that we don't have all the answers. And when authenticity and vulnerability come together in harmony, they create resonance—a deep, echoing connection that touches others, reminding them of their own truths, challenges, and triumphs.

We will explore the heart of these concepts. It will shed light on why it's crucial, now more than ever, to embrace these qualities in our transformational journey. Through heartfelt stories, introspective reflections, and actionable insights, we'll understand how showing our most genuine self, with all its fragilities, can profoundly connect us with the world around us. Let's discover the power of being real, raw, and resonant.

Vulnerability Unveiled

Vulnerability is one of the most profound aspects of the human spirit. It is a window into our souls and a bridge that connects us. But what does vulnerability really mean? Why does it cause us to feel so many different emotions? At its core, vulnerability is the act of exposing oneself emotionally, of allowing oneself to be seen. It's about removing the armor we so carefully crafted and letting the world see our scars, fears, hopes, and dreams. It's a state of being that is simultaneously terrifying and liberating.

Yet, in our modern world, vulnerability is often misunderstood. As mentioned, many perceive it as a sign of weakness, a crack in the armor that others might exploit. But this couldn't be further from the truth. Vulnerability is an act of immense strength. It requires courage to show our true selves, especially when society often demands a facade of perfection. It's an act of rebellion against the norm, a testament to the strength of our spirit.

But if vulnerability is empowering, why do we shy away from it? The answer lies in the societal constructs and values ingrained in us. From a young age, many are taught to be strong, to hide their tears, to mask their emotions. "Don't let them see you cry" is a mantra many have heard. These societal pressures, combined with our internal fears of rejection or judgment, create barriers that prevent us from expressing our true selves.

Yet, as we will discover in this chapter, embracing vulnerability can lead to profound connections and transformative experiences. It's a journey into the heart of our humanity, a deep dive into our emotional core, and a bold step toward authenticity and resonance.

The Rewards and Risks of Vulnerability

On one side, there lie the enriching rewards—intimate connections, self-awareness, and a path to healing. On the other, the looming risks—potential misinterpretations, unsolicited judgment, and the raw exposure of our emotional selves. It's a delicate balance, but understanding the rewards and risks can empower us to tread this path with grace and wisdom.

First, let's explore the rewards that vulnerability can bring to us. When we dare to bare our souls, we invite others to do the same, fostering more profound, meaningful connections. This raw honesty allows relationships to flourish, moving beyond the superficial to touch the core of our shared human experience. In the process, we often discover profound truths about ourselves.

By confronting our fears, insecurities, and aspirations openly, we begin a journey of self-awareness, recognizing our strengths and areas of growth. Additionally, vulnerability offers healing from past traumas and pains. By sharing our stories, we often find comfort in the empathetic embrace of others, realizing we're not alone in our struggles.

However, like all powerful forces, vulnerability comes with its share of risks. When we open up, we make ourselves susceptible to misinterpretations. Our stories, when shared, can be viewed through the lenses of others, sometimes leading to unintended conclusions or perceptions. Furthermore, not every environment or individual is receptive to raw honesty. Judgment, apparent or subtle, is a risk every vulnerable individual must be prepared for. And, of course, there's the undeniable risk of emotional exposure—of revisiting wounds or sharing parts of ourselves that we've kept hidden.

So, how does one navigate? The key lies in balance and discernment. It's essential to recognize that vulnerability is not a one-size-fits-all approach. While it's a powerful tool for connection and growth, it's equally important to set boundaries. Knowing when to open up and when to protect oneself is crucial. This isn't about building walls but understanding that vulnerability, like all aspects of our lives, requires context.

Authenticity

At its core, authenticity is about being genuine, true to oneself, and not fake. It means sharing experiences as they are, not as we think they should be. In storytelling, this translates to presenting stories with all their raw edges, unpolished corners, and genuine emotions. While today's world is full of stories that are polished to perfection and tailored to cater to a particular image or audience, there's an unmistakable magnetism in stories that are authentically shared. These stories tug at heartstrings, coming from a place of genuine experience and emotion.

Perfection, while aesthetically pleasing, often lacks depth. The narratives that show a 'perfect' image can be distant or unrelatable. On the contrary, raw authenticity invites readers or listeners into a shared space of understanding and empathy.

Now, when authenticity merges with vulnerability, storytelling transforms into an art form. Vulnerability adds layers to authenticity. It is the courage to showcase the imperfections, the challenges, and the growth. Authenticity ensures the story remains true, while vulnerability gives it depth and dimension. Together, they create narratives that are not just heard but felt.

The Magic of Empathetic Storytelling

Every story holds the potential to move, inspire, and connect. However, stories told with empathy have an added layer of magic.

They don't just recount events; they make listeners and readers feel seen, heard and understood. Empathetic storytelling is forging a deep emotional connection, transcending words on a page or sounds in the air.

Empathy, at its core, is about understanding and sharing the feelings of another. When incorporated into storytelling, it transforms narratives from basic accounts into soulful journeys that resonate profoundly with the audience. But how does one infuse empathy into a story? It begins with a genuine intention to connect, to understand, and to honor the feelings and experiences of others.

One of the most effective techniques for weaving empathy into a narrative is to put oneself in the shoes of the listener or reader. Consider their perspective, their life experiences, their hopes, and their fears. How would they feel hearing or reading your story? What elements would resonate most deeply with them? By anticipating and respecting these emotions, storytellers can craft narratives that are not just impactful but also deeply touching.

Additionally, details matter in empathetic storytelling. Vivid descriptions and emotionally charged language can draw the audience in, making them feel like they're living the story with you. Understanding and respecting the emotions and experiences of the audience is fundamental to empathetic storytelling. This means being sensitive to potential triggers, avoiding stereotypes, and honoring diverse perspectives.

Empathetic storytelling is both an art and a skill. It requires intentionality, insight, and a genuine desire to connect. But when done right, it can create narratives that linger in hearts long after the last word is read or heard. Through empathy, we don't just share stories; we bridge souls, and in doing so, we highlight the shared humanity that binds us all.

Tips and Techniques for Genuine Storytelling

The world is saturated with stories—from 280-character tweets to epic novels—but what makes a story stand out is its genuine nature. Let's look into the practicalities of crafting genuine narratives.

Connect with Your Core:

Authenticity begins with self-awareness. Before penning down your story, analyze your mental, emotional, and spiritual state. Understand your motivations, your feelings, and the message you want to convey. Dive deep into your reservoir of emotions and memories, and don't shy away from the uncomfortable or raw ones. It's often in these untouched, vulnerable spaces that the most genuine stories emerge.

Show, Don't Tell:

One of the golden rules of storytelling is to show rather than tell. Instead of stating feelings or events, paint a picture with words. Let the readers find emotions through actions, dialogues, and surroundings. This immersive technique allows readers to engage actively with your story, forging a deeper emotional connection.

Stay True to Your Voice:

Every storyteller has a unique voice and style. Embrace yours. While it's natural to be inspired by others, mimicry often leads to diluted authenticity. Your experiences, perspectives, and emotions are unique, and they deserve a unique voice.

Avoid Over-embellishing:

While a touch of drama can elevate a story, overdoing it can strip away its genuine nature. Aim for balance. Let the emotions and events in your story shine without burying them under excessive flair or exaggerated details.

Seek Feedback:

Share your stories with trusted individuals before presenting them to a wider audience. Constructive feedback can offer invaluable insights, helping you refine your narrative and ensuring it remains genuine while resonating with your intended audience.

Stay Open to Evolution:

As we grow and evolve, so should our stories. Authenticity in one chapter of our lives may look different in the next. Allow your stories to breathe, evolve, and adapt. This flexibility not only ensures continued genuineness but also keeps your narratives relatable and fresh.

Avoid Stereotypes and Generalizations:

While universality in themes can enhance resonance, resorting to clichés or stereotypes can create disconnects. Treat each character and scenario with the depth it deserves, steering clear of oversimplified portrayals.

Reflection

As we close this chapter on authenticity, vulnerability, and resonance, it becomes evident that the heart of impactful storytelling lies in the raw, unfiltered truths we choose to share. When we embrace our vulnerabilities, stripping away the facades and revealing our authentic selves, our stories gain an undeniable power to connect, heal, and inspire.

Throughout the chapter, we've journeyed through the complexities of vulnerability, understanding its strengths and potential pitfalls. We've explored the essence of authenticity and how it forms the soul of any resonant narrative. Each account, each lesson, serves as a testament to the profound impacts that stem from embracing and sharing our vulnerabilities.

Embrace your unique journey with its highs and lows, joys and pains. Recognize the strength found in vulnerability and the depth of connection it can forge. Wear your vulnerabilities with pride, understanding that they are not marks of weakness but badges of authenticity.

Lastly, as you craft and share your narratives, strive to resonate. Understand that in every story you tell, there lies the potential to touch a heart, change a perspective, or even transform a life. Your story, with its raw emotions and genuine truths, is a gift—a gift that, when shared, has the power to create waves of empathy, understanding, and inspiration in the vast ocean of human experience.

11

— • —

INSPIRATION AND IMPACT

On a day that seemed like any other, destiny had other plans. A six-year-old girl, dusky, fragile, and gasping for breath, was hurried into the emergency room. With my background in pediatric intensive care, my colleague and I were called in to take on this difficult challenge. Yet, as the minutes ticked by, we realized that the depth of this trauma went beyond our preparatory experiences.

Our trauma room was not available as it was being sanitized when the child arrived on scene; time was running out with limited resources available to us. The child, despite her young age, had already faced numerous medical interventions, having knocked on two urgent care doors only to be handed steroids and bronchodilators. Still, no clear diagnosis had been provided on how best to address her health problem.

We engaged in a fierce battle for what felt like an eternity, but it was just over two hours. Stationed at her bedside, I found myself locked in a silent exchange with her—her eyes, clouded with fear yet shining with hope—met mine as I whispered words of hope, encouraging her to find the strength to endure. We tasted momentary triumph when she revived, but fate had other plans as she soon slipped away from our grasp.

Desperation led us to seek expertise beyond our immediate surroundings, but destiny had the final say. The weight of her loss was one I carried, a truth that surfaced months later when our medical director sought understanding into that night. I could not control my emotions; I broke down in tears at this discovery.

Post-mortem revelations pointed to a respiratory illness distinct from the dreaded Coronavirus. Yet, in the thick of our efforts that night, the dots had connected differently, hinting at a potential link to Wuhan, China, owing to her familial ties. Every resource and every ounce of expertise was poured into her care, but some outcomes, tragically, remained unchangeable.

This heart-wrenching episode, while a testament to the vulnerability of life, also illuminates the profound impacts our interactions can have. The name of that little girl, the unforgettable image of her gaze, and the anguished cries of her family are imprinted on my soul. Her tragic story has served me as a lesson to the ripple effects of our actions and experiences, serving as a guide for inspiration and impact.

Life often operates in cycles. Much like the rhythm of nature, where the change of seasons happens in a predictable yet ever-fascinating manner, human experiences are governed by a similar pattern, especially regarding inspiration and impact.

It's fascinating to observe how individual growth isn't a solitary journey. When a person undergoes transformation, the ripples of that change extend beyond themselves, touching lives and, in turn, inspiring others. This sets off a cycle. Someone's moment of enlightenment can serve as a motivator for another, who then becomes a torchbearer for another. We will explore the relationship between the individual and the collective. How does one's personal journey of change inspire and drive change in their community, and how does the evolution of the community shape individual trajectories?

The Inspire-Impact Loop

Every individual, knowingly or unknowingly, is part of a continuum that constantly sways between inspiration and impact. Think of it as a loop where a single spark of inspiration can lead to transformative actions, which inspire others to begin their journeys of change. This cycle, which we'll call the "Inspire-Impact Loop," is the core of how humans propel themselves and those around us toward growth and evolution.

At the foundational level, this loop is energized by two primary forces: intrinsic and extrinsic motivators. Intrinsic factors are deeply personal, arising from within an individual. They could stem from one's values, beliefs, aspirations, or passions. For instance, a personal setback might inspire someone to develop resilience, and their journey of overcoming obstacles can impact and motivate others facing similar challenges.

On the other hand, extrinsic factors originate from external sources. These could be societal norms, peer influences, cultural trends, or global events. For example, witnessing a community come together in the face of adversity can inspire an individual to contribute positively to society, creating an impact that further fuels collective inspiration.

Navigating this loop requires a sharp sense of awareness. One must recognize moments of inspiration, harness their potential, and channel them into impactful actions. Simultaneously, remaining receptive to the transformations is essential, as they often hold invaluable lessons and inspirations. The magic lies in understanding that this cycle is never static; it's always in motion, with every moment of inspiration and every act of impact feeding into the next, creating a powerful cascade of growth and change.

The Personal-Communal Bridge

This intertwining relationship between the personal and the communal is similar to a bridge, where one's experiences, learnings, and growth resonate outwards, impacting the collective consciousness. The foundation of this bridge is built upon empathy. Personal growth often involves overcoming challenges, learning from failures, and celebrating successes. As we navigate these experiences, we develop a deeper understanding of human emotions and struggles. This refined sense of empathy allows us to connect more profoundly with others, offering support, understanding, and guidance based on our experiences.

Communication is the roadway on this bridge. By sharing our stories, insights, and lessons, we allow others to learn from our journeys. Every act of communication has the potential to touch lives. Individuals can find comfort, inspiration, and direction through these shared experiences.

Active engagement is the bridge's pillar, giving it strength and stability. It's one thing to grow personally and another to proactively use that growth for the betterment of the community. This could involve mentoring, volunteering, launching community initiatives, or simply being there for someone in need. By being actively involved, we ensure that our personal evolution doesn't remain in isolation but seeps into the community, creating positive ripples of change.

The Personal-Communal Bridge signifies that personal growth isn't a self-centered effort. When channeled effectively, it has the power to transform societies. As communities evolve, they, in turn, foster environments that jump-start individual growth.

Nurturing a Community of Change Makers

At present, it has never been more pressing to foster change-makers. Individual works, while impactful, amplify when united within a community effort. To establish such a transformative community, we must do more than gather passionate individuals; we must cultivate an ecosystem that promotes growth, innovation, and transformation.

A thriving community's heart lies in its environment. By promoting open dialogue, we build bridges of understanding and mutual respect. Creativity blossoms when community members feel heard, and their ideas are validated. Additionally, by celebrating victories, we inspire further innovation. Yet, acknowledging and learning from setbacks is just as vital; they are the stepping stones to success.

Mentorship, in this context, emerges as a crucial component. Pairing developing enthusiasts with experienced change-makers facilitates the transfer of invaluable insights. While structured mentorship programs can guide this process, we shouldn't underestimate the power of peer-to-peer learning. Often, learning from someone on a similar journey, a few steps ahead, can offer relevant and immediate insights.

At the heart of every impactful change-maker is a strong support network. This isn't just about having a shoulder to lean on during challenging times, though emotional support is crucial. It also involves sharing vital resources like tools, contacts, or books, which can significantly accelerate one's journey. Furthermore, combining strengths through collaborative projects can broaden the scale and reach.

Challenges in Maintaining Momentum

Every cycle of inspiration and impact will face its share of obstacles, no matter how powerful or transformative. Just as a bicycle needs regular tuning to ensure smooth pedaling, so does the inspire-impact loop need maintenance to sustain its momentum.

The first challenge many encounter is the flow of personal motivation. While the initial burst of inspiration can feel invigorating, maintaining that enthusiasm in the face of day-to-day realities can be intimidating. Distractions, competing priorities, or simply the weight of routine can slowly dilute the initial spark. Furthermore, setbacks and failures, an inevitable part of any journey, can cast a shadow of discouragement, causing many to question their path or even abandon it altogether.

Beyond individual struggles, external challenges can also intervene. Resistance from the community, changes in the socio-political landscape, or shifting economic tides can all throw a wrench in the most well-laid plans. And then there's the challenge of scalability. What begins as a personal mission can grow; as it does, the challenges of managing larger teams, securing resources, and expanding impact can come to the forefront.

However, these challenges, while tough, are manageable. In fact, they offer valuable learning experiences. To keep the momentum alive, it's crucial to develop resilience. One way to achieve this is by consistently revisiting and repeating the source of one's inspiration, anchoring oneself in the 'why' behind the journey. Regular reflection and setting short-term achievable goals can provide consistent motivation.

Moreover, seeking support is vital. Whether from mentors, peers, or a dedicated community, sharing challenges and collectively brainstorming solutions can lead to breakthroughs that remain unseen in isolation. Embracing a growth mindset that views challenges as learning opportunities rather than impossible barriers is also important. And, when faced with external roadblocks, flexibility can be a potent tool. Adapting strategies, rerouting plans, or even taking a step back to reassess can often prove more fruitful than strictly sticking to a predefined path.

Ensuring Continued Inspiration and Growth

The journey of inspiration and growth is not a sprint but a marathon. It demands sustained effort, a reservoir of motivation, and the continuous nurturing of the spirit. Certain practices and principles can serve as guiding lights when navigating, ensuring that one remains rooted while still reaching for the stars.

To begin with, individuals must recognize that inspiration is not always a blazing inferno; sometimes, it's a gentle ember. Keeping that ember alive requires nourishment. This is where self-reflection plays a key role. Journaling, meditation, or even simple walks in nature can offer the solitude necessary for self-reflection.

Continued learning is another cornerstone of sustained growth. The world around us is in a state of endless evolution, and to stay relevant and inspired, one must be willing to become a student. This could mean attending workshops, reading, or seeking diverse experiences that challenge existing worldviews and expand horizons. The abundance of inspiration remains fresh by constantly adding to one's knowledge and experiences.

But the most profound sustenance for enduring inspiration is staying connected to one's core values and mission. In the noise and chaos of life, it's easy to get sidetracked, to lose sight of the 'why' behind our actions. Revisiting this 'why' through personal mission statements, vision boards, or core value lists can act as a compass, steering us back when we drift too far from our intended path.

In addition to these practices, surrounding oneself with like-minded individuals who share similar aspirations or challenge us positively can reignite passion. These connections remind us of our purpose, mirroring the impact and importance of our journey.

From Local to Global

The phrase, "Think globally, act locally," captures a fundamental truth about the power of localized efforts. While global change can feel intimidating, small, local initiatives often ripple outwards, creating waves of transformation that extend far beyond their point of origin.

Consider the humble beginnings of many major global movements. They usually start as localized efforts, born out of a specific need or challenge within a community. However, their underlying message or solution often resonates universally, leading to more expansive adoption and impact. It's a testament to the interconnectedness of our world, where a single spark can ignite a wildfire of change.

Take, for instance, the environmental movement that began with small community initiatives. Witnessing firsthand the detrimental effects of pollution or deforestation, local groups initiated conservation efforts. As these actions and their benefits became more visible, they were adopted by neighboring communities, eventually gaining momentum to influence national policies and global treaties. The story of the plastic bag ban, which started in a few towns and now spans multiple countries, is a fitting example.

Another case is the campaigns for education rights in underprivileged areas. Local activists, recognizing the transformative power of education, initiated community schools or tutoring programs. These localized efforts drew attention to the larger systemic issues, leading to global campaigns like Malala Yousafzai's fight for girls' education, which started in Pakistan and resonated globally.

The boundary between the local and the global is penetrable. Localized inspirations, fueled by authenticity and genuine need, possess a universal language. They tap into shared human experiences, aspirations, and challenges, making them relatable and adaptable across varied contexts.

In light of this, it becomes evident that every local effort, no matter how small, has the potential for global impact. By addressing specific community challenges with passion, innovation, and resilience, individuals and groups can lay the foundations for broader changes. Their stories, once shared, can inspire similar efforts elsewhere, perpetuating a cycle of inspiration and impact that knows no geographical bounds.

Reflections

A beautiful truth lies at the core of inspiration and impact: one person's growth, discovery, and resilience journey can spark community transformation. On the other hand, the collective efforts of a community can uplift and inspire individual journeys.

What's more profound is that this cycle knows no bounds. Its ripples can extend from the personal to the communal, from the local to the global. Like a stone tossed into a still pond, the circles of impact widen, touching shores far and beyond. Each story of change, each act of courage, and each moment of authentic vulnerability adds to this ripple, creating numerous testimonies.

You are both a product and a producer in this inspire-impact loop. Your journey holds immense power with unique challenges, breakthroughs, and lessons. By sharing it, acting upon it, and channeling its purpose, you contribute to a narrative of change.

As you stand at the intersection of personal growth and community impact, remember you are never alone. Every step you take, every story you share, and every hand you extend joins a chorus of voices and actions striving for a better world. Together, we can amplify the echoes of inspiration and impact, ensuring they resonate through time and space.

12

BUILDING A LEGACY OF TRANSFORMATION

In the final chapter of this book, I want to talk about legacy in the context of personal transformation. It's a moment to pause and reflect, embodying the profound realization that "You'll never be happier than you are grateful." This simple yet powerful statement isn't just a fleeting thought; it's a pillar of the transformative process, a guiding principle that shapes who we are and the legacy we leave behind.

Throughout this book, we've explored various facets of transformation—from uncovering our core truths to reshaping our thoughts and sharing our stories of change. Each step on this path hasn't just been about personal growth but how it extends beyond our individual lives. It's about how our journey, struggles, and victories can touch and inspire others. Our transformation is the legacy we are building—a legacy that's not just about what we do but also about who we become.

But what exactly is a legacy? When we think of legacies, our minds often leap to magnificent ideas—monumental achievements, lasting institutions, leaving behind large monetary assets to family, or significant societal contributions. While these are undoubtedly aspects of legacy, a legacy is much simpler and more personal at its core. It's the imprint we leave on the world through our daily actions, choices, and interactions. It's the warmth we bring into the lives of those around us, the inspiration we spark in others, and the positive changes we foster in our communities. It's about living a life that reflects gratitude, joy and uplifts and empowers.

Consider the concept of gratitude and how integral it is in shaping our legacy. Gratitude is more than just a feeling of thankfulness; it's a mindset, a way of seeing the world. It's about recognizing and appreciating our blessings despite challenges and hardships. This perspective of gratitude can transform our inner world and our external interactions. When we approach life with a heart full of gratitude, we radiate positivity, kindness, and compassion. These qualities, in turn, profoundly impact those around us.

Our legacy, therefore, is linked to our journey of personal transformation—a journey marked by self-discovery, growth, and a deepening sense of gratitude. It's about using our experiences, knowledge, and insights to make a positive difference. It's about how we embody the values we cherish.

As we discuss the concept of legacy, it's important to understand that our legacy isn't just about the milestones we achieve or the accolades we receive; it's about the lives we touch, the hope we instill, and the positive changes we help start. As we venture into this discussion, we will reflect on how we can craft a legacy that aligns with our deepest values and aspirations. Let's remember that at the heart of our transformation and the legacy we aspire to build lies our capacity to be grateful.

The Legacy of Personal Transformation

Personal transformation as a legacy surpasses any material inheritance. It's an evolution that, when deeply rooted in gratitude, extends into the lives of those we touch, creating a lasting impact that transcends time and material possessions.

"Did you get your Vitamin G today?" This question is not talking about physical nutrition but more in the realm of spiritual sustenance. Vitamin G, representing Gratitude and God, is about nourishing our souls with a sense of thankfulness and a connection to God. It's about daily recognizing the "get-to's" in our lives, anchoring us in a state of contentment and appreciation.

Imagine a family where one member begins their transformation strengthened by gratitude. This change can ripple through the family, altering relationships. A parent's shift towards a grateful mindset can inspire children to cultivate the same, fostering a family environment where appreciation and acknowledgment are common. Such transformations can lead to a more harmonious home where each member feels valued and connected.

Beyond family, the impact of personal transformation resonates through friendships and community networks. A grateful individual often emerges as a source of positivity, their presence uplifting those around them. The power of gratitude lies in its simplicity and ability to transform everyday interactions into moments of connection and joy.

Grateful people approach life with a sense of abundance, focusing on what they have rather than what they lack. In a world fixated on material gain and individual success, gratitude brings us back to the root of what truly matters: relationships, experiences, and the joy found in everyday life.

Reflecting on whether we've had our daily dose of Vitamin G reminds us to pause and appreciate life's blessings. By nurturing a heart of gratitude, we contribute to the well-being of our family, friends, and community, leaving behind a legacy that outlives material possessions. The legacy of personal transformation, therefore, is not measured in tangible assets but in the unforgettable mark we leave on the hearts and minds of others. It's about how we've helped shape their perspectives and enriched their lives. As we navigate our transformation paths, let us embrace gratitude as a fundamental element, understanding that our legacy is not just about what we leave behind but also about the change we instigate in the world around us.

Creating a Multi-Generational Impact

Vitamin G' encapsulates more than just gratitude; it represents a trio of vital components that nourish our soul and spirit. First, there is "Time With God," a sacred moment of surrender, allowing God and wisdom to guide our paths. When shared and observed within a family, this spiritual connection instills a sense of faith and trust in the higher power, providing a foundation of strength and hope for future generations.

Next comes the "Get-to List," a transformative shift from viewing life's tasks as burdens (have-tos) to opportunities (get-tos). This perspective change is crucial. When we approach daily responsibilities with gratitude, seeing them as chances for growth and learning, we teach our children, grandchildren, or anyone who may look up to us the power of a positive outlook. This attitude turns everyday moments into lessons of resilience and appreciation.

Lastly, there is the principle of "Giving Self Grace." During our transformation phase, we must remember to be gentle with ourselves. Embracing this principle means acknowledging that progress isn't always a straight line and that setbacks are inevitable. By modeling this self-compassion, we teach younger generations to treat themselves and others with kindness and understanding, an invaluable lesson in today's fast-paced world.

When we take our dose of Vitamin G daily, we create a legacy that echoes through generations. Children and grandchildren who grow up in environments where gratitude is a daily practice, challenges are seen as opportunities, and self-compassion is a norm will carry these values forward.

Moreover, these practices of gratitude and growth go beyond shaping individual characters; they mold family dynamics. A family that practices gratitude fosters a culture of appreciation and mutual respect. Sharing stories of challenges overcome and lessons learned becomes a way of bonding, offering guidance and wisdom to the younger members. These stories, enriched with lessons of gratitude, become a legacy, cherished and passed down through storytelling, traditions, and shared experiences.

Utilizing our unique talents and passions for the betterment of others is another way to build our legacy. Whether through artistic expression, sharing knowledge, or lending a skill, using our gifts to enrich others' lives brings personal fulfillment and adds depth and richness to our legacy.

Moreover, how we nurture and maintain relationships forms an integral part of the legacy we leave. Our interactions, characterized by empathy, understanding, and gratitude, create lasting impressions on those we connect with. We establish a legacy of love, respect, and meaningful connections by valuing these relationships.

By embedding gratitude, resilience, and self-compassion into our daily lives, we equip our future generations with tools for a fulfilling life. Our legacy becomes one of emotional and spiritual richness, a guiding light for generations to come, and a testament to the enduring power of 'Vitamin G' in shaping lives. Along with embracing opportunities for growth, practicing kindness, sharing our talents, and cherishing relationships, we create a legacy that leaves a lasting, positive imprint.

Crafting Your Legacy

Crafting your legacy narrative involves articulating and envisioning the long-term impact we wish to have, with gratitude and self-reflection as our guiding lights.

To start crafting your legacy narrative, begin with gratitude. Reflect on the experiences, people, and circumstances that have shaped your journey. Acknowledge the challenges that have strengthened you and the joys that have enriched you. Gratitude isn't just about feeling thankful; it's about recognizing the connection between your life experiences and how they contribute to your legacy.

Next, consider the impact you want to make. What do you want to be remembered for? How do you want to influence your family, community, or world? Your legacy doesn't have to be monumental—it could be the kindness you spread, the resilience you embody, or how you uplift others. Use these reflections to shape a narrative that includes the passion in your life's work and values.

To help you define your legacy, here are some exercises and prompts:

1. **Gratitude Mapping:** Create a visual map of your life's journey, highlighting moments of gratitude. Include people, events, and experiences that have significantly impacted you. This map will serve as a reminder of the many blessings in your life and how each has contributed to your legacy.

2. **Legacy Statement:** Write a statement that explains the legacy you wish to leave behind. This statement should reflect your values, the impact you want to make, and how gratitude shapes your perspective. For example, "My legacy is to inspire and nurture resilience in others, guided by a heart full of gratitude for every life experience."

3. **Daily Legacy Actions:** Identify small actions you can take daily to live out your legacy. These could be simple acts of kindness, moments of self-reflection, or steps toward a larger goal. Remember, no matter how small, every action contributes to your legacy.

4. **Letters to the Future:** Write letters to your future self, children, a future generation, etc. Express your hopes, wisdom, and the lessons you want to pass on. These letters are a living expression of your legacy.

Remember that your legacy narrative is not set in stone as you engage in these exercises. It's a living, evolving story that grows as you do.

Sustaining Your Legacy

Sustaining a legacy is an ongoing process that requires patience, perseverance, and a profound understanding of the nonlinear nature of progress. There will be highs and lows, successes and setbacks. It's crucial to give yourself grace during this process. It's about nurturing the seeds of transformation you've planted and ensuring they continue to grow and flourish, even during challenges. The nonlinear path is not a sign of failure but a natural progression of any meaningful endeavor.

Strategies for Sustaining Growth and Impact

1. **Reflect Regularly:** Take time to reflect. Acknowledge your growth, celebrate your achievements, and learn from your challenges. This regular reflection helps you stay aligned with your legacy and adapt as needed.

2. **Stay Grounded in Gratitude:** In moments of doubt or struggle, return to gratitude. Remember the phrase, "I am breathing, I am a child of God, I am blessed." This mindset will help you stay focused on the positive aspects of your journey and the impact you're making.

3. **Seek Support and Community:** Sustaining a legacy can be challenging in isolation. Seek a supportive community or a mentor who can provide guidance, encouragement, and a different perspective when needed.

4. **Revisit and Adjust Goals:** As you evolve, so will your vision of your legacy. Adjusting your goals and strategies to align with your current realities and aspirations is okay.

Sustaining your legacy is an ongoing process. It's about constantly aligning your actions with your core values, embracing the ups and downs, and remaining committed to making a positive impact. Throughout these pages, we've explored the depths of personal transformation. We are on the verge of turning our newfound insights into lasting legacies.

Reflection

Personal transformation extends far beyond individual achievements. It's about the legacy we leave behind, the imprint we make on the lives of others, and the values we instill in future generations. This transformation journey is marked not only by the changes we undergo but also by the impact of these changes.

At the heart of this transformation is the power of gratitude. The simple yet profound practice of taking our "vitamin G"—nourishes our souls, shifts our perspectives, and shapes our actions. It's a reminder to appreciate the blessings in our lives, no matter how small, and to see each day as an opportunity for growth and contribution.

Our transformation is a testament to the idea that redefining our legacy is never too late. Whether it's mending strained relationships, seeking forgiveness, or starting anew, each step we take is a part of the story we leave behind. It's about crafting a story that reflects our growth, struggles, and victories. This story showcases how much we've changed and our positive influence on those around us.

As you continue on this path, let your daily declarations (for example; love, patience, sobriety, humility, and integrity) guide you. These are not meaningless words but commitments to a way of being that elevates your life and the lives of those you touch. They form the foundation upon which you build your legacy—a legacy of transformation that transcends material possessions and symbolizes hope and inspiration.

Step forward with confidence and purpose, knowing that your transformation journey is continuous, filled with endless possibilities and endless potential. Embrace the future with an open heart and a grateful spirit, and let your story of change and growth continue to unfold. You have the power to create a legacy that resonates for generations. Your legacy awaits, and the world is richer with your presence in it.

— · —

Trauma to Triumph

Last year my pastor shared the
shame and guilt he once held.

Standing still, I knelt down,
for that's when my heart began to melt.

As I walked past the podium
that morning to ask for wisdom and prayer.

The Holy Spirit revealed my purpose,
like peeling onions, layer by layer.

At my core, I declare myself, "Love".
Reparented by my Heavenly Father.

Just last year, I felt like a pig on a conveyor belt,
preparing to get slaughtered.

I suffered mentally and emotionally
from Post Traumatic Stress.

Depression robbed me of all my joy,
cuz life was one huge mess.

(Sigh) So here's my story, brothers and sisters,
I'll try to keep it brief.

Basically, what I do for work
is to help other people breathe.

The 24th of February, the year
was two thousand and twenty.

I went to the Staples Center that morning
to pay respects to Gigi and Kobe.

Sobbing, I was filled with grief
in a stadium full of adoring fans.

Short lived, hopped on a plane,
had to work that night, Yo...I was exhausted, man.

Got to the hospital, I was RT assigned
to care for adults, in the ICU.

Strange, I thought, past 2 years I've been working
with tiny humans in the NICU.

Room 3113, laid a woman on a ventilator.
Simply, she was sicker than sick!

Going downhill fast, organs failing,
with lungs that were stiffer than bricks.

Part of my job is caring for souls, at their deepest,
darkest, most vulnerable state.

Not taking work home is like getting older,
eating crap expecting to gain no weight.

My next day off, I'm in The City,
at the game between the Warriors and Lakers.

My boss calls, patient has Coronavirus.
I was lit, like a diffused circuit breaker.

The first community acquired Corona case
in the whole United States.

Looking back, it was then that the Lord
began to make my crooked paths straight.

Dozens of lives, I witnessed, held hands,
with those who would die all alone.

Lord, use me, in these troubled times,
to help bring your people home!

Every day on the job, in the face of fear,
I clocked in, felt like I was going to war.

Emotions held in: sorrow, guilt and grief,
didn't know that the body keeps-score.

I shunned out others, smoked and drank.
Daily I was numbing and denying.

The enemy was working overtime,
the master of deception and gaslighting.

Bitterness, defeat, then rage!
I was spinning and spinning,
like a never ending cycle.

Empowered one day, lonely the next,
laid depressed. Desperate for spiritual revival.

Search my heart! I cried out to Him.
"Why did you bring me all the way here?!"

Be still, He said. But I couldn't though.
My shame had me dripping, in fear.

Suicidal from unbearable anxiety.
You left the 99 in search for lil ol' me.

A son, two daughters, my beautiful wife
and a home, oh how good and faithful is He!

You sent your soldiers to fill me up,
when my spiritual tank was running on E.

Gave me just enough, I rely on YOU.
You are the planter, and I am your tree.

Lord, what shall I do, I need your love!
What if my boss calls me a liar?

He whispered, the tree that's planted by the water...
isn't phased by the FIRE.

You sure this is what you want for me,
Lord, how long is this pain gonna last?

Son, A heart that's planted in forgiveness
doesn't dwell on the past.

God provided all our needs and then some.
He filled me with His mercy and grace.

Taxing trials turned into a triumphant testimony.
You saved this warrior, named Ace.

Because of you Lord, I declare myself
SOBER, PATIENT, INTEGRITY and HUMILITY.

I recover out loud so that your name is glorified,
cuz you never let my past ruin me!

You sacrificed your only begotten son,
Jesus shed blood to forgive all my sins.

Every breath I take is a gift from you.
Holy Spirit, my council within.

—·—

CONCLUSION

T he Trilogy of Triumph—truth, transformation, and testimony—has been the backbone of this book. This framework has led us through the stages of personal growth and self-discovery. Each stage, an important pillar in its own right, has contributed to a holistic understanding of what it means to transform and impact the world around us.

Recounting the Trilogy of Triumph

In revisiting these core pillars, we begin with truth. This initial stage was all about peeling back the layers, uncovering the masks we wear, and reconnecting with our true selves. It was a process of reflection and honesty, where we confronted our deepest fears, insecurities, and dreams. Truth served as the foundation, the starting point of a journey that would take us to places within ourselves we might have been hesitant to explore.

Then came Transformation, a stage marked by active change and personal evolution. The transformation stage was where the insights and realizations from our pursuit of truth began to take shape into real shifts in our thoughts, behaviors, and actions. Transformation was about applying what we learned, experimenting with new ways of being, and embracing the discomfort that often accompanies growth. In this stage, we began to see the fruits of our labor, the emergence of a new self, resilient and more aligned with our core values.

Finally, testimony is the stage where our personal stories of change and growth are shared with the world. This was about embracing vulnerability, authenticity, and the power of our stories to inspire and resonate with others. Testimony was not just about celebrating our triumphs but also about acknowledging the struggles, the setbacks, and the lessons learned along the way. It invited others to begin their transformation journey, fueled by our courageously shared stories.

Each stage of the Trilogy of Triumph is connected, feeding into and strengthening the other. Truth led to transformation, and transformation paved the way for testimony. Together, these stages form a continuous cycle of growth and impact. This journey does not have a definitive end but evolves and unfolds as we navigate the complexities of life.

I hope these insights and lessons from this trilogy remain with you as you progress, guiding your steps and choices. Transformation is an ongoing process, a lifelong pursuit of becoming the best versions of ourselves and making a meaningful impact on the world. Let's carry forward the spirit of the Trilogy of Triumph, embracing each day as an opportunity to learn, grow, and inspire.

Moving Forward

Life's trials and tribulations are not barriers to our journey; they are stepping stones, each one leading us closer to understanding ourselves and the world around us more profoundly. These challenges are essential to our growth, pushing us to explore new depths of our resilience and strength.

This ongoing journey is a process of constant evolution. As we move through different stages of our lives, we are presented with new situations and experiences that challenge our existing beliefs and push us to grow in new directions. We understand who we are and what we can contribute to the world with each step.

As you move forward from this book, remember that your journey is unique and precious. It is a journey of becoming, of unfolding into the fullest expression of yourself. You have the power to shape your path, to make choices that align with your most profound truths, and to create a life that resonates with your highest aspirations.

So, as you close this book and step into the next phase in your life, do so with courage and hope. Remember that you are not alone on this path; we are all travelers on the same road, seeking our truths and striving to make our mark on the world. Embrace your journey with all its twists and turns, for it is in this unending path of growth and discovery that we find our true selves and greatest potential.

This book is more than just a collection of words and concepts; it's a call to action, an invitation to apply the lessons learned to your daily life. Each chapter and idea has been a stepping stone towards understanding and embracing your core truth, fostering personal transformation, and preparing to share your impactful testimony with the world.

Acting on your insights means taking concrete steps to implement the strategies and exercises discussed throughout the book. It involves making intentional changes in your life, whether adopting new habits, letting go of old ones, or simply shifting your mindset. Remember, transformation begins with action, no matter how small.

Reflection is equally important. It's a process of continual self-assessment, asking yourself if your actions align with your core truths and the goals you've set for yourself. Reflecting on your journey helps you understand your progress, celebrate your victories, and learn from your setbacks. It's an ongoing dialogue with yourself, ensuring you stay true to your path and purpose.

Thank you for being on this journey with me. Your engagement, willingness to dive deep into your mind, and courage to face your truths have been invaluable. This book is just the beginning; the real transformation unfolds in your life beyond its pages.

Remember the power lies within you. The power to change, grow, inspire, and impact the world in ways only you can. Keep shining your light, for in doing so, you brighten your path and light the way for others to transform trials into testimonies!

-Blessings and love, Ace

Thank you for joining me on this journey. If you would like to connect, email me at ace@aceaspiras.com

Made in the USA
Las Vegas, NV
19 July 2024